ARNOLD BE   . &
FREDERICK MARRIOTT

PARALLEL LIVES

JOHN SHAPCOTT
Keele University

CHURNET VALLEY BOOKS
1 King Street, Leek, Staffordshire. ST13 5NW 01538 399033 www.leekbooks.co.uk
©John Shapcott, University of Keele, and Churnet Valley Books 2019
ISBN 9780995603998

The parallel lives of Bennett and Marriott began at 6 Netherton Grove

CONTENTS

INTRODUCTION

The catalyst for this book was an exhibition held as part of the 2018 English Tourism Week. The Barewall Gallery in Burslem, Stoke-on-Trent, devoted their exhibition space to an impressive display simply titled *Frederick Marriott Etchings*, but one which left the intriguing question 'Who was Peter Frederick Marriott?' unanswered. When he is remembered at all today it is not so much for his artistic merits, but rather for the memoir he wrote of his friend Arnold Bennett, *My Association with Arnold Bennett*. The original holograph is held in the University of Keele's Special Collection Archive and was published by the University in 1967 to mark the anniversary of Bennett's birth in 1867. I have long valued my copy of this booklet as providing important, often detailed, information about Bennett's early years which might otherwise have been lost. Subsequent Bennett biographers have mined it for valuable insights unavailable elsewhere. Seeing the booklet displayed in the Barewall exhibition space made me decide to revisit the Keele holograph to see just what had disappeared in those sections of the published version marked '[Omission]'. The answer turned out to be nearly everything that related directly to Marriott, his personal quirks and, importantly, his artistic credo and methodology.

Minor, but nonetheless productive and interesting lives, all too often fall beneath the biographer's radar. One such personality was Peter Frederick Marriott, who has never totally escaped from the shadow of his great friend Arnold Bennett to take on an independently celebrated textual life. Yet without Marriott's remembrance of life with Bennett, especially the shared experiences of young men hoping to make an impression on the world of art and literature, we would have lost a unique insight into the cultural life of the late-Victorian and Edwardian world. It is admittedly difficult to assess the significance of peripheral lives and to justify time spent on delving into lost time, but I am conscious of George Eliot's conclusion to *Middlemarch* where she speaks of the ordinary everyday life of her heroine Dorothea:

> Her finely-touched spirit had still its fine issues, although they were not widely visible.... the effect of her being on those around her was incalculably diffusive: for the growing good of the world is partly dependent on unhistoric acts; and that things are not so ill with you

and me as they might have been, is half owing to the number who lived faithfully a hidden life, and rest in unvisited tombs.[1]

At the time of writing I know exactly where Bennett's tomb is located in Burslem and could visit it from my home in less than 30 minutes. I have a copy of Marriott's death certificate and know that he died on 2 October 1941 in Shrewsbury, but as to the exact location of his tomb or ashes I have no idea. What I do have is the conviction that Marriott brought happiness to his artistic friends, especially to Bennett, at the same time as quietly pursuing a worthwhile and professionally successful life. Of this life little has been recorded. This book is not then a standard biography of one man, but rather an attempt to flesh out details of Marriott's artistic and social skills through restoring the missing sections of his *Memoir* whilst taking the opportunity to cross-reference his comments in alternate chapters with previously not readily available material on his friend Bennett. My hope is for a greater appreciation of both men, and a desire to encourage others to uncover yet more information.

For me, the journey of discovery very much began at that Barewall exhibition, and with one etching in particular. I admired Marriott's 1922 etching of the medieval town of Carcassonne, so much so that a print now hangs in my study. Determined to find out some background I discovered that Marriott began a life-long affection for France from the moment he was first taken there by Bennett. And Bennett was certainly impressed by Carcassonne, as can be seen from his journal entries, a *Country Life* article, and a laudatory fictional citation:

'M. Laugier came from Carcassonne, and was proud of his origin'. (*Imperial Palace* [1st edition], p.385).

'I should say that (except Carcassonne, of course) Vezelay, in the Avalonnais, is perhaps the most picturesque town in all France. Chateau Landon comes near it, and is much easier to get at'. ('A Feudal Town in France', in *Country Life*, 19 December 1908, p.887.)

'This morn. We came straight through Bèziers to Carcassonne, 146 k. In $3^3/4$ hours over indifferent but straight roads. I had quite a wrong idea about Carcassonne. I thought the town itself (30,000 inh.) was a monument. However, the cité as restored by Viollet le Duc is highly curious. Also church therein. Hotel Moderne. Good'. (*Journal*, 28 April 1914, in: NF 11, p.87/Berg Collection).

'Arrived at Hotel Tivollier [Toulouse] at 11 [...] having left

Marriott's Carcassonne etching

Carcassonne at 8.45. Excellent hotel at Carcassonne, thoroughly well run, but socially and aesthetically suffering from complete absence of chambermaids. The whole thing is done by men'. (*Journal*, 29 April 1914, in: Berg Collection).[2]

And then, as if to leave no doubt that I was destined to further explore the allure of Marriott's Carcassonne etching, the writer Kate Mosse published the first novel of an intended trilogy, *The Burning Chambers* (2018)[3] set in and around medieval and modern Carcassonne. Looking at Mosse's back catalogue I came across her 2005 novel, *Labyrinth*[4], a historical fiction also played out in the medieval and contemporary Carcassonne. Not only did it prove to be an engrossing read, but the title *Labyrinth* suggested itself as precisely the exegetical biographical maze I was about to enter in searching for the somewhat elusive Frederick Marriott.

In approaching Marriott and Bennett in such a personally involved way I take some comfort from Graham Holderness's reflections on the art of biographical enquiry: 'Biography should be emotionally involved, not dispassionate; self-reflective, not neutral; experimental and innovative, not realist and documentary. In addition, a biography should be metabiographical, explicitly telling the story of the biographer's engagement with the subject'.[5] Certainly Marriott was happy to link his life with that of Bennett, espousing any notion of biographical distance or impartial objectivity, with the happy result of giving us a warm and intimate portrait.

One significant reason why Peter Frederick Marriott's biography resists easy recovery is that it has become confused with that of his younger brother, Frank Pickford Marriott. Various internet sites have muddled the two brothers' identities and their art works, to create a labyrinthine puzzle. Indeed, one such site, goldenagepaintings.blogspot.co.uk, creates a hybrid artist named Frederick Pickford Marriott, before then wrongly assigning the 1900 painting *Faithful Knight* to Peter rather than Frank Marriott. Attempting to separate the two biographies I have been greatly assisted by Alan Grobler sending me the 2008 issue of *Looking Back: The Journal of the Historical Society of Port Elizabeth* (Vol. 47, 2008). In it, his article 'Frank Pickford Marriott, A.R.C.A., A Post Pre-Raphaelite'[6] gives a comprehensive history of Frank's association with the Port Elizabeth School of Art from 1903 until his death in 1935. More importantly, Grobler gives an insight into the early collaborative efforts of the two brothers that may help account for some of the identity confusion. For instance,

...together with his elder brother Frederick (1860-1941), he produced work in mother-of pearl (the nacre or inside lining of a shell) and gesso (a mixture of plaster of Paris and a glue size, which formed a basis on which to paint). Gesso was widely used by the early Italian masters of the 15th century in the preparation of religious panels. The work produced by the Marriott brothers later became recognized as being prime examples of the Art Nouveau/Arts and Crafts movement in England.[7]

Frank Pickford was born 10 June 1876, in Coalbrookdale, Shropshire. He emigrated with his parent's family to Australia, where his father, Samuel, was commissioned to assist with the construction of the Brisbane Bridge, whilst his brother Frederick remained in England. (This Australian connection was later to prove central to Frederick's family life.) Meantime, Frank left school early to supplement the family's income by working in a jam factory. This seemingly blind alley had a happy outcome when Frank's artistic talents were let loose on designing product labels. At this point Frederick's sense of family loyalty becomes apparent when he encourages and assists his brother's return to England to complete his studies in art at Onslow College of Art, London, in 1890. Recommended by Walter Crane for the post Art Master at the School of Art in Port Elizabeth, Frank arrived in South Africa in October 1903, returning only once to England to marry Hannah Winifred Andrews (1880-1964) in 1908. At this juncture, the two brothers take separate paths.

Our brother, Frederick, was born 20 October 1860 in Fenton, Stoke-on-Trent, thus giving the first, if somewhat tenuous, link with his great friend to be, Arnold Bennett. (The family home was at Mount Pleasant, close to the railway where his father was employed as an engineer.) Tenuous, because he soon moved with his parents to Shropshire; although we further note that both Marriott and Bennett had relocated to London before the age of twenty-one. There is a further uncanny link with Bennett -- born in Hanley in 1867 but brought up in Burslem -- who set much of his early fiction in Burslem while omitting Stoke-on-Trent's sixth town of Fenton from his fictional Five Towns[8].

To digress for a moment, so as to make amends and relocate Bennett's Fenton, and Marriott's birthplace, on the literary map. The renowned Argentinian philosopher and story writer Jorge Luis Borges chose Bennett's comic novel *Buried Alive* (1908) as one of his favourite books, to rank alongside more obvious choices such as *A Thousand and One Nights*, Robert Graves's *Greek Myths* and Henry James's *The Figure in the Carpet*. This choice is perhaps not so surprising when we recollect that Borges's paternal grandmother, Frances Haslam, was born in Stoke-on-Trent (1842), later emigrating to Argentina, taking with her a love of English writers. In her revelatory exploration of Borges's literary inheritance and his ancestral ties to Stoke-on-Trent, *Red Thread*, Charlotte Higgins quotes from Borges's autobiographical sketch remembering his grandmother as 'a great reader. When she was over eighty, people used to say, in order to be nice to her, that nowadays there were no writers who could vie with Dickens and Thackeray. My grandmother would answer, "On the whole, I rather prefer Arnold Bennett, Galsworthy and Wells"'.[9] When Borges's takes the narrator of his 1941 labyrinthine story 'The Garden of Forking Paths' to Fenton I am inclined to read it not only as an acknowledgement of his grandmother's influence but also as restitution for Bennett's consigning the town to literary oblivion. And to round off this unexpected conjunction of fact and fiction in Fenton, Frederick Marriott dies in the very year Borges's story was published.

Frederick Marriott received his early training as an apprentice at the School of Art at Coalbrookdale. By the age of 14 he had begun work as a pottery painter at Maw & Co.'s factory at Jackfield, Shropshire, manufacturers of tiles and earthenware. Frederick felt justifiably proud of painting several of the firm's exhibits for the Paris Exhibition of 1878. A year later, in 1879, he not only gained a National Scholarship at the Royal College of Art, but also gained the rare distinction of becoming one of the first students to have their scholarship extended to three years in recognition of outstanding talent.

On leaving the Royal College of Art, Frederick obtained the post of designer and illustrator for the firm of Marcus Wood & Co, where he built up a thorough knowledge of the processes of lithography and printing that were to serve him so well in later years. From there he moved to a more lucrative appointment as Chief Designer at Eyre & Spottiswoode, remaining with them for four-and-a half years. This London based firm of printers and publishers began in 1878 producing Christmas cards on an industrial scale but which nevertheless retained an elegance of design, thanks no doubt in part to Frederick's aesthetic good taste. To date I have found two very attractive surviving examples of his illustrative book art at this time, both published by Eyre & Spottiswoode: the cover design and internal illustrations for Charlotte M. Yonge's *Nurse's Memories* (1888) and Sarah Wilson's *Children's Prayers* (1887). Alisa Clapp-Itnyre writes that the latter: '... boasts vivid illustrations, framed by small, inlayed flowers

and branches, with idyllic images of English estates and praying girls'.[10]

Incidentally, Frederick's curtailing of his name to 'Fred.' was a not uncommon practice at the time, although he reinstated the full spelling as editor of *The Universal Art Series* for the publishers Chapman & Hall in the 1920s. I might also take this as an opportune moment to note that Frederick and Bennett both dropped their first given names - Peter and Enoch respectively - favouring their middle names for the whole of their professional lives.

By 1905, Marriott could claim to have had practical experience in all branches of design for applied art, having executed commissions for the following industries: Furniture, Wall Papers, Lithography, Metal Work, Bookbinding, and Stained Glass. Such a wide-ranging curriculum vitae would surely have recommended him to the equally multi-talented Bennett.

With this body of practical work to recommend him it is not surprising that Marriott was in demand to move into the world of teaching. His first major post was as Design Master at Blackheath Art School. He was next appointed as Headmaster of the Onslow College of Art School. From there he became the highly influential and innovative Headmaster of the prestigious School of Art, Goldsmiths' Institute, New Cross, holding the post for 30 years from 1895-1925. We have some indication of the high esteem in which Frederick was held during his tenure at Goldsmiths' College, and of his role there, from an article published in the September 1918 issue of *The Studio Magazine*, number 306 - 'The Goldsmiths' College School of Art' by Malcolm C. Salaman, pp.118-125.[11] Salaman describes the College's move under Marriott from being a largely craft inflected institution to one giving way 'to the artistic, and a

very flourishing and influential centre of art training it has become'
(p.118). Salaman goes on to emphasise Marriott's central role at the time:
'Here study is pursued in the evening as well as the daytime, and under
the general direction of Mr. Frederick Marriott, the well-known painter,
gesso worker, and engraver, who, with foundation of the school, started
the design class, and has been Head Master for the last twenty-five years...'
(Ibid.). Most importantly, Salaman emphasises Frederick's sympathetic
and stimulating fostering of the etching and engraving side of the
College's artistic work. He also includes a number of etchings to illustrate
his article and to demonstrate the students' increasing skill in etching
techniques at representing facial expression and character 'under Mr.
Marriott's helpful auspices' (p.124).

All this time Frederick continued to produce his own work, gaining
a growing reputation from fellow artists. His work was exhibited at the
Royal Academy, New Gallery, Arts & Craft Exhibition, and the principal
provincial galleries. His range of techniques on display included oil-
painting, etching, mezzotint engraving, and panels in modelled gesso and
mother-of-pearl inlay. (Frederick goes into further detail about the
technical side of his work in my restored passages of his Bennett *Memoir*.)
Some of his works have been reproduced in *The Studio*, *The Art Journal*,
The Magazine of Art, *The Architect*, and *The Building News*, and today they
are increasingly to be found on the internet. Given his many
accomplishments it comes as no surprise to find that he was made
Honorary Associate of the Royal College of Art, was a member of the
Arts and Crafts Society, and Member of the Art Workers' Guild. But
Frederick took particular pleasure in realizing the high esteem in which
he was held by his fellow practitioners by being elected acting Chairman
of the Society of Art Masters.

Unfortunately very few of Bennett's letters to Marriott have been
published, and the 18 or so references to time spent with him in Bennett's
published journals deal almost exclusively with the early years of their
friendship. Perhaps surprisingly none of these touch upon Marriott's
artistic talent and so we cannot turn to Bennett for an insight into any aspect
of his artistic career. There is, however, one unfortunate exception to this
lacuna. In his memoir *Arnold Bennett: A Last Word*,[12] Frank Swinnerton
records what he refers to as frequent exchanges of 'quite silly little jokes'[13]
between himself and Bennett, one of which concerned Frederick:

We were driving into the celebrated Garden [Cintra] when I saw an unexpectedly familiar sight. I exclaimed 'Good heavens! I've seen a vista of this picture painted by the worst artist in the world! Bennett asked 'and who is the worst artist in the world?' I told him, 'Stanley Inchbold', and he said 'Oh, no, he's not the worst artist in the world. The worst artist in the world is my old friend Frederick Marriott'.14

Such 'silly' jokes committed to print many years after the event convey none of the camaraderie in which they were made.

In fact, the true value of Marriott's artistic output is now slowly becoming apparent. Tim Crook's on-line *Goldsmiths History Project,* with a substantial section devoted to Marriott's time there, as well as mentioning his friendship with Bennett, represents an important addition to our understanding of his development as artist and teacher. Crook reproduces Harold Speed's official Goldsmiths' College portrait of Marriott, painted in 1925, and hung in the College conference room before disappearing from sight and gathering dust in storage.

Harold Speed's portrait of Marriott

I was particularly pleased to track down an article by Philippe Garner in *The Bulletin of the Decorative Arts Society 1890-1940,*15 published in 1977, but seemingly now forgotten. In it, Garner devotes most space to Marriott's own unpublished notes on the technique of working in gesso, but he also gives an insightful sketch of Marriott's output in the context of the times, and of his artistic relationship with his brother Pickford. Garner has absolutely no doubts about the significance of Marriott's contribution to early twentieth-century art forms:

A curious and somewhat paradoxical product of the great craft revival of the last quarter of the nineteenth century was the rediscovery and exploitation of the craft of gesso [chalk or plaster]. The paradox lay in the unhappy contrast between the guiding principles of the Arts and Crafts Movement and the bewitching decadence which characterises the work of the two artists who achieved the finest results in gesso. The two masters of the medium were Frederick Marriott and

Margaret Macdonald Mackintosh, and both created their finest pieces in the first years of the twentieth century.[16]

Angel of the Night

Garner became interested in learning more about Marriott when a group of his panels came up for auction at Sotheby's in 1968, together with manuscript documentary material which included his lecture notes. *The Angel of the Night*, executed in gesso and mother-of-pearl is a typical example of Marriott's opulent panels that cannot help but call to mind Russian iconic art.

Equally opulent is his depiction of Oberon looking, in Garner's words, 'resplendent in shimmering winged armour of mother-of-pearl'[17]. This image can boast a continuing afterlife in contemporary popular culture since it was selected to feature on the album cover of Barclay James Harvest's 1976 vinyl album *Octoberon* and the subsequent re-mastered 2003 compact disc. The three disc CD/DVD special edition released in 2017 features Marriott's *Oberon* over the fold out three page album/disc sleeve. Harvest's cover harks back to a specific Edwardian period in Marriott's career when there was a strong urge emanating from the Arts and Craft movement to recapture the romance of medieval symbolism and the 'whimsy of the fairy tale'[18] .

In his lecture notes, reprinted in Garner, Marriott describes the lengthy research and methodology employed to achieve the astonishing wonderful colours and their iridescent qualities displayed in his panels. For example:

In a translation of an old Italian book I found that a permanent purple stain for marble mosaic was obtained from chloride of gold, so I got some from a chemist and put some pieces of shell into the solution, but it had no effect at all. Then I tried the effect of boiling the shell in the solution, with the result that it produced a purple of extraordinary

Oberon/Octoberon

richness ....I followed up this experiment by boiling pieces of shell in other colours, blues, reds and yellows, with equally good results, so there seems to be no limit to the range of colours possible..[19]

Little wonder then that Marriott was regarded as such an inspirational teacher, able to enthuse his students with his own ever-developing interest in new techniques.

At the same time as Marriott was engaged in the Art and Crafts Movement's revival of medieval ideals of craftsmanship he continued to paint everyday subjects in oils and watercolour. A particularly delightful example of this, with the added attraction of its provenance, is his small (25/35 cm.) oil painting of trees, believed to be in the neighbourhood of Marriott's Chelsea home.

This is an oil painting on canvas and board, which, when first purchased at auction 'looked dull and without any expression'

15

(DasPasKuntst1.blogspot.com). It wasn't until careful cleaning that Marriott's subtle depiction of light nuances on the tree bark, creating a sense of perspective, was revealed. The wooden panel to which the picture was stuck carries the scribbled but clearly legible legend 'F. Marriott. 6 A Netherton GNove (sic) Chelsea SW 10'. And this was the house and studio where Marriott first met and began his life-long friendship with Bennett.

But what prompted Marriott to write his very personal and affectionate account of his time with Bennett? The answer is to be found in a two page handwritten document held in the Keele University Archive, which Marriott titled *Adventures with Arnold Bennett: Introduction*. It begins: "'And now Sir, to business. I want you to write a book about your adventurous times with Arnold Bennett. Come and have lunch with me and we'll talk about it". This quotation, from a letter I received from my friend Mitchell Kennerley explains how this little book came into being'. Mitchell Kennerley was the brother of Bennett's brother-in-law, W.W. Kennerley. Marriott was clearly impressed by Bennett's fellow-man from the North, writing of his:

> ...truly astonishing rise from the modest position of junior salesman in a publishing office, to the eminence of one of the leading publishers in America [Doubleday], and head of an important company of Art Dealers.... Another distinguished production of 'The Five Towns', for Mitchell Kennerley was born in Burslem, and in common with Arnold Bennett, he presented the traditional North Staffordshire characteristics of energetic and forceful frankness.

Kennerley and Marriott:

> ...discussed the proposition for the 'Adventures' during lunch, & afterwards to the accompaniment of cigars and liquid refreshment. Under such circumstances it is not surprising that I was persuaded to devote such time as I could spare from my own to recording any incidents of general interest I could recall which had happened during my long friendship with Arnold Bennett.

There is no obvious reason as to why the manuscript was not published by Doubleday, although we know from an exchange of letters between Bennett and his literary agent in 1930[20] that Bennett was considering whether to continue with his American publisher. There may also have been an element of doubt as to the commercial prospects for the memoir in the economic Depression years of the 1930s following Bennett's death, when his literary reputation was under re-evaluation from the Modernists.

Published now in its entirety, alongside my selection of other fascinating but rarely seen Bennett work, we have the opportunity to enhance our understanding of both men's careers in the context of their times. Each of Marriott's memoir chapters (odd numbers) elicits a response from me (even numbers) to create a hybrid form of biography offering a fresh and enlarged perspective on turn-of-the-century literature and art.

So, let us return to that scrawled and misspelt oil painting address of 6A Netherton Grove and that fateful meeting.

A young Arnold Bennett. c. 1905

Watercolour of Bennett,
M. du Mayne, 1891.

1. FIRST MEETING

It was in the Autumn of 1890, during the progress of an evening party at the Blackheath home of Mr. Joseph Hill, (the founder and Head Master of the local School of Art and Crafts) that I first met Arnold Bennett. He was about twenty two years old, but appeared to be younger, partly I think, on account of his lavender-coloured voice, and high-pitched boyish laughter.

He had recently arrived in London from Burslem, to take up work in the offices of a firm of solicitors, and Hill, being a native of Burslem, and a great friend of Bennett's parents, Arnold's visits to Hill's house were fairly frequent.

I soon discovered that he was interested in literature, art, and music, and I invited him to come and spend an evening in my Chelsea studio, which I had built but a short time previously. He came the following week, and that was the commencement of a staunch and unbroken friendship, extending over a period of forty years.

I had bought an eighty-five years lease of my house No. 6, Victoria Grove, (since renamed Netherton Grove) off the Fulham Road. Joined on to the back of the house I had built the studio, which took up a good portion of the garden.

The cost of the lease, and the building of the studio, not only absorbed all my savings, but compelled me to raise a mortgage of £400. Now this mortgage weighed heavily on my mind, and caused me many restless nights, for I was so inexperienced in matters of business in those days, that in spite of the excellent security the value of the property provided, I felt horribly ashamed of being in debt to the extent of £400, and I practiced the most rigid economies in an endeavour to clear off the mortgage as quickly as possible, but with my limited income it was naturally a very slow process.

During one of Bennett's subsequent visits, it transpired that he contemplated changing his lodgings; so after he had gone, my wife propounded the brilliant idea of inviting him to come and live with us as a paying guest.

The title of paying guest as applied to lodgers had then but recently been coined: to make it possible for the lower middle and professional classes to increase their limited incomes by letting rooms without hazarding their self respect.

Appropriate and discreet negotiations were immediately set on foot which brought about the desired result, and one fine day Bennett arrived in a cab heavily laden with his goods, a huge case of books forming the mightiest portion. The cabby gave a hand in unloading and carrying the luggage into the house, and Bennett's installation was successfully completed.

After tea, he immediately set about the business of unpacking his cases, and rearranging his rooms. One of his first difficulties was to find accommodation for his books, for we didn't possess a book-case equal to the strain of such a quantity. So I suggested having shelves put all round his sitting room up to the height of the dado moulding. This was done, but he insisted on defraying the whole of the cost, although I protested that it was really my business to provide the accommodation.

Among the things he bought with him was his own clock, which occupied the centre of his sitting room mantel-shelf. In the panel on the base of the clock he had printed in Roman capitals, "DO IT NOW.", which was an indication of the thorough type of student he was.

It was his own suggestion that he should pay his rent in advance; an arrangement which was accepted without argument, and thus he became a valuable contributor to the Marriott mortgage redemption fund.

He took his meals with us, and it was his habit at that time to read during their progress, particularly at breakfast time; propping his book or magazine up against some convenient object on the table. I don't know whether he persisted in this time-saving custom in recent years.

It was a pleasant discovery that he could play the piano, and particularly that he liked playing accompaniments, for I prided myself on having a tenor voice of some quality. Indeed, at one time, on the advice of friends, I had serious thoughts of taking up singing as a profession, and enrolled as a student at the Kensington School of music (now the Royal College) with that idea; but I soon found that it was an impossibility for me to earn a living at art and have sufficient time left for the serious study of singing. In short, it was a hopeless task to try and carry on two full-time jobs.

However, I enjoyed singing, and Bennett enjoyed playing, and with his good taste and knowledge of music he was very helpful to me; not only in introducing me to new songs, but also in keeping me in practice with the songs I already knew. These intervals of musical recreation with Arnold Bennett live in my memory as some of my pleasantest experiences. He had already formed the habit of devoting some portion of each day to piano practise, and he kept it up to the end.

I was very glad to have a companion in the house who was an indefatigable worker, and who was sympathetic towards my work; and I found him very helpful both with suggestions and criticisms.

We took frequent walks together along that favourite promenade, the Chelsea Embankment, and through the old parts of Chelsea, and I well remember his interest in the accounts I gave him of some of my early experiences when I first came to London in 1879, to take up my National Art Scholarship at South Kensington, while Sir Edward J. Poynter R. A. was Principal. How, one day when on my way to school, I had seen Thomas Carlyle driving down Oakley Street and had followed the conveyance to watch him alight and enter his house in Cheyne Row. Also, that one morning as I was going up the art school stairway, I passed the picturesque figure of the poet Tennyson in his wide brimmed sombrero hat and long Inverness cloak, and carrying in his hand a 'church warden' clay pipe; my juvenile curiosity compelling me to wait in the corridor while he entered Sir Edward Poynter's studio, to give a sitting for his portrait.

One day, as we walked past the house on the Embankment in which Turner the great landscape painter lived and worked for some years, Bennett was greatly interested when I told him a story I had heard the veteran painter Horsely tell at a meeting of the Art Worker's Guild; Horsely said that when he was a young man, he had sat next to Turner at a dinner party, and had been told by him that he hadn't missed seeing the sun rise for thirty years. By the way, the iron pallisading which Turner had caused to be erected round the flat roof of the house, to give him greater security while studying sun-rise effects, can still be seen in position, and there is a bronze tablet on the front of the house to denote that the great painter had lived there.

Horsely, speaking of Turner's amazing out-put, stated as a fact, that although he attained a ripe old age, there is a sketch, or a finished picture in existence for every day he lived. A testimony of Turner's unflagging industry, which I believe is without parallel in the history of art. It much impressed Bennett.

Occasionally, during our rambles round Chelsea, Bennett would halt to enter a brief note in one of the small note books it was his custom to carry for the purpose of recording any unusual happenings, or anything of particular interest. Later on this developed into his practice of keeping a more complete journal, and at Christmas 1906, he published the first of a series of small books, limited to a hundred copies each, under the title of THINGS WHICH HAVE INTERESTED ME, BEING LEAVES FROM A JOURNAL KEPT BY ARNOLD BENNETT. These little books were printed at Burslem by Joseph Dawson, a bookseller, stationer and printer, and were given by Bennett as Christmas gifts to his relatives and friends. Happily, I am the possessor the three published in the years 1906, 1907 and 1908.

Sometimes on Sunday afternoons, we used to visit the studios of Mr. G.F. Watts R.A., and Sir Edward Burne Jones A.R.A., which were open to the public. There were not only finished pictures displayed, but works in various stages of progress were on view, (standing on easels,) clearly demonstrating the methods of procedure and technique of these two painters, making them particularly interesting to young students.

As evidence of Bennett's strict sense of duty, the following incident of those early days is worthy of record.

One evening as he was going out to the post, my wife asked him to post her weekly letter to her people, and she said, 'Arnold, I hope you don't neglect to write to your Mother every week.' He answered, 'My dear lady, I write to my Mother every day, and I tell her everything I think will interest her. She knows everything that happens in this house'. I believe he followed this practice consistently as long as his mother lived.

For a considerable time after he began to send articles to the various papers and magazines, the bulk of his work was returned with disconcerting regularity, accompanied by the usual stock expressions of regret in use by editors.

On one of these occasions I remember saying to him 'Have you drawn another blank Arnold?' To which he replied, 'Yes, but I'll make them have 'em.' And he did.

He was incessantly charging against difficulties of some kind, and enjoying the exercise. He stubbornly refused ever to acknowledge defeat.

In course of time, Arnold Bennett's youngest brother, Septimus, won a National Scholarship for modelling, tenable at South Kensington for two years, and Bennett proposed that we should let him rent half the house and engage his own servant, in order that his brother could come and live with him.

He offered more generous terms than we should have asked, or than he would have had to pay for similar accommodation elsewhere. His first experiences of house-keeping were not without thrills.

He engaged as general servant an ex-sailor named Fish; a very appropriate name in view of after events.

Fish made an admirable start, working well and efficiently for the first few days, and we were all satisfied that he was a treasure. However, on the Saturday morning, just before Bennett left for the office, he gave Fish a few instructions and a sovereign, for the purchase of the weekend provisions. After the lapse of an hour or so, during which he tidied up the rooms, Fish left the house, sovereign in hand, and was never seen again by any of us.

It was a remarkable coincidence that the name of the next servant Bennett engaged was Pond, also an ex-sailor, who proved to be a thoroughly capable and trustworthy man.

He kept the rooms scrupulously clean and tidy, and was an excellent cook. He was not exposed to the severe temptation that brought about the down-fall of Fish, for he was never given sovereigns to shop with. Pond was such a success, that one of Bennett's friends facetiously remarked that it would have been better if he had got his Pond before his Fish.

No. 6 Netherton Grove
(Victoria Grove).

2. MEET THE MARRIOTTS

The studio of Frederick Marriott's that Bennett rented has remained little changed over the years. When the freehold went on the market in 1981 it was valued at £160,000, and the estate agent's blurb thought it worthwhile in marketing terms to include the promotional detail that the 'Studio, which is linked to the main house, was once used by Arnold Bennett, novelist playwright and critic'.[21] The sale particulars describe Bennett's studio annex in some detail - suffice it to say here that the bathroom boasted William de Morgan tiles, and that the south-facing patio was surrounded by trees and was completely secluded.

On the evidence of the *Memoir* we can thank Marriott for not only introducing Bennett to the work of a range of contemporary artists but, even more importantly, of accompanying him on visits to their studios. Margaret Drabble writes of how the Chelsea of Marriott's day 'enjoyed a fine reputation for artistic life... there were still lots of working artists around: Sargent, Whistler and Wilde all lived there and so did William de Morgan, Walter Sickert and Wilson Steer'.[22]

Bennett himself saw this as a golden period in his artistic education, recording in his autobiography *The Truth about an Author*:

> I was enabled to take up my quarters in the abode of some artists at Chelsea. I began to revolve, dazzled, in a circle of painters and musicians who, without the least affectation, spelt Art with the majuscule; indeed, it never occurred to them that people existed who would spell it otherwise. I was compelled to set to work on the reconstruction of nearly all my ideals. I had lived in a world where beauty was not mentioned, seldom thought of.... Modern sideboards were called handsome, and Christmas cards were called pretty, and that was about all. But now I found myself among souls that talked of beauty openly and unashamed.[23]

The Sunday visits to Edward Burne-Jones's studio strike me as being of major literary importance when we recall that it was Burne-Jones's work that was to spark in Bennett an epiphany, or flash of insight, that was every bit as important as his more critically commented upon response to the 1910 Post-Impressionist exhibition in influencing his literary credo. Bennett's *Journal* entry for 3 January 1899 leaves me in no doubt that he was searching for a literary technique that would echo changes in painting, one that I believe finds full modernist fruition in novels such as *The Pretty Lady* (1918) and *Riceyman Steps* (1923):

> At the Burne-Jones Exhibition; ... The sight of Burne-Jones's aloofness, of his continued preoccupation with the spiritual, to the ignoring of everyday facts, served to complete in me a modification of view which has been proceeding now for a year or two. The day of my enthusiasm for 'realism', for 'naturalism', has passed. I can perceive that a modern work of fiction dealing with modern life may ignore realism and yet be great. To find beauty, which is always hidden; that is the aim. If beauty is found, then superficial facts are of small importance. But they are of some importance. And although I concede that in the past I have attached too high a value to realism, nevertheless I see no reason why it should be dispensed with. My desire is to depict the deeper beauty while abiding by the envelope of facts. [24]

At the time of this entry we see Bennett inching towards this search for an essential beauty in the everyday with his turn to symbolic realism via the referencing of some of the artists brought to his notice by Marriott. Early examples would include Whistler and Sickert in *A Man from the North* (1898), Holman Hunt in *Anna of the Five Towns* (1902), and G.F.Watts in *The Sinews of War* (1906).

Noticeable by his absence from the artists that Marriott mentions is that of Simeon Solomon, and I cannot help but conjecture that Marriott may have been a little over-censorious and sensitive about drawing attention to him. Christie's 2018 auction 'Sale Notes' calls Solomon 'the greatest Victorian artist you've never heard of'. Exhibiting at the Royal Academy at age 18 he goes on to become a leading light of the Pre-Raphaelite movement, his contemporary Burne-Jones calling him 'the best of us all'. But his career never recovered from his arrest in 1873 for a homosexual act and a sentence of imprisonment, later commuted to a £100 fine. From there ensued a downward spiral of drunkenness, poverty and homelessness that ended with his death in the workhouse at age 64.

It is inconceivable that Marriott was unaware of Solomon's exquisite engravings and Bennett certainly knew about him, and would have been conscious of the later parallel case of Oscar Wilde. Solomon's output is now being rediscovered and re-evaluated - see Clare Barlow's 2018 study *British Queer Art, 1867-1967* and Colin Cruise's 2005 *Love Revealed: Simeon Solomon and the Pre-Raphaelites* - and to my mind Bennett's 27 November 1897 Journal entry merits its place as an interesting foot-note on this rehabilitated master-painter:

> Indirectly I heard news of Simeon Solomon through a picture dealer in Regent Street, via Marriott. Simeon Solomon was once one of the lights of the Pre-Raphaelite school, the friend of Rossetti and Burne-Jones, who both had sincere admiration for his work. The dealer said that he was now in a lunatic asylum. 'At one time' he said, 'I gave him £2 a week and took the sketches. The money was paid daily, for he was always penniless'. Marriott asked where Solomon lived in those days. 'He didn't live anywhere', the dealer said; 'he had no home. If he could afford it he slept at a common lodging-house; if not, on the Embankment'.
>
> Marriott said that Solomon had really been mad for years, and that many years ago, it was stated that he was reduced to doing sketches for pots of beer.[25]

Here we see two friends, Bennett and Marriott, in everyday conversations about the vicissitudes of the art world, conversations that were typical of the new world, far from the Potteries, that Bennett now inhabited.

Simon Solomon's 'The Haunted House' - 'The greatest Victorian artist you've never heard of.'

3. THE POTTERIES

With the approach of Christmas, we received a cordial invitation from Bennett's parents to go to Staffordshire with him and spend the holidays with the family. This we readily accepted, and in due course we were merged in the annual Christmas exodus from London at an average speed of about fifty miles an hour.

It is common knowledge, that where the great manufacturing industries are situated in the British Isles, invariably there will be found some of the most beautiful scenery in the country. Such is eminently the case with the group of manufacturing towns known as The Potteries, for they are set in the midst of a richly wooded undulating stretch of landscape of great beauty, and the people who live in these towns are justly proud of their fertile environment.

This great industrial group has been immortalised in the novels by Arnold Bennett as 'The Five Towns'.

I had always been interested in the Potteries, the more because I happen to have been born there, but I generally think of Shropshire as my native county, for circumstances conspired to remove me from Stoke-on-Trent, my birthplace, to St. Georges in Shropshire when I was barely three months old, and it is strange that it was not until I met Arnold Bennett, thirty years later, that I got my first opportunity of visiting it again.

Arnold's father met our train at Stoke, and we were quickly conveyed to his home in Waterloo road, Burslem, where we got our first introduction to the exuberant hospitality which is one of the characteristics of the people of North Staffordshire.

Mr. and Mrs. Bennett, and every member of the family conspired to make our first holiday in the Potteries thoroughly enjoyable, and we formed many lasting and valued friendships there.

A vivid impression remains of the elaborate preparations for the Christmas Day festivities. First there was a generous distribution of festoons made of laurel and ivy leaves, with focus points of holly and mistletoe, combined with bright coloured Chinese lanterns arranged according to a scheme which had been previously discussed and carried into effect by the younger members of the household.

A huge Christmas tree, freely covered with sparkling decorations and loaded with gifts, was illuminated by small coloured candles in the approved fashion. Books and other presents too bulky to be attached to the tree were arranged on a side table.

The means for making music were not wanting, for there was an American organ in the dining room and a piano in the drawing room, and every member of the family had been taught to play. Frank, the second son, played brilliantly, and took as keen an interest in music as did Arnold.

Sons and daughters alike were practiced in Choral singing, and were all good readers of music. Tertia, the youngest of the three daughters was the chief vocalist, and possessed a voice of exceptional quality and purity of tone, and I believe that if she had had the advantage of training with a good professor, and had taken up singing as a profession, she would have made a name.

A Christmas party at the Bennetts was a stupendous affair, and the room in which it was held was filled to overflowing with relatives and friends of the family, and was a typical example of the warm-hearted generous hospitality, for which, as I have said before, the people of the Potteries have a well merited reputation.

Arnold Bennett was the chief organiser, and his personal qualities of thoroughness and foresight were manifest. Nothing was left to chance where he was concerned in the management. He arranged the programme of entertainment which followed the distribution of presents from the Christmas tree, and as I had a budding reputation as a raconteur and mimic, I was included in the list of entertainers.

Bennett had repeatedly seen my mimicry 'turns' and he knew the stories I had in my repertoire, so before the entertainment was timed to start, he handed me a slip of paper giving the titles, and the order in which they were to occur. A good indication of the practical and orderly features of his composition.

****

RESTORED TEXT

In several of my mimicry stories, there occurred imitations of the mannerisms and accent of Church Parsons. The following is one of those included in the programme.

In a remote country village there was a delicate Parson who was rather idle and casual in the matter of clerical duties, and he deputed to Robinson, the verger, the reading of the Church notices at the Sunday services!

Robinson combined the offices of Verger, Sexton and Grave-digger, and he was very proud of being allowed to read the Church notices.

After a time the old Parson became too feeble to carry on, and a young energetic Vicar was appointed in his place, who immediately started making changes to the service.

One of the most important changes was to introduce 'Hymns Ancient and Modern' in place of the hymn books he found in use. Moreover, he strongly objected to Robinson reading the Church notices. But on seeing Robinson's bitter disappointment, he consented to his reading any unimportant ones, so he gave him the notice about the change of Hymn books to read. Now, Robinson was very deaf, and on the following Sunday, when the Vicar, reading out the notices said, 'Dearly Beloved, I propose on Sunday next, to hold a baptismal service in the Church at three o'clock in the afternoon, and I desire them to attend with their babies at the time appointed'.

Putting his hand up to his ear, Robinson said, 'Why, he's giving out my notice about them Hymn books!' Then, in a very loud voice he said, 'And them what haven't got 'em, can have 'em by applying at the vestry, ordinary a shilling, and extra strong with red backs eighteen pence!'

****

It was the jolliest and most successful Christmas party we had experienced. There were no blank passages, no waiting for suggestions as to what to do next, for a continuous variety entertainment of games and music had been carefully planned beforehand, and everything was carried out with the most exuberant good humour.

This was the first of a number of Christmas parties it was our good fortune to attend at the Bennetts, and at the homes of other friends in the Potteries, where hospitality never fails.

It did not take us long to discover what remarkable people Arnold Bennett's parents were. Their sterling qualities made an indelible impression upon us, and immediately an affectionate and enduring friendship was established between us.

I gathered that Arnold's father originally worked as a potter, and it is evidence of his persistency and forcefulness of character, that after he was married and had a young family, he embarked on the study of law, and determined to qualify as a solicitor. It was in his father's office in Hanley that Arnold Bennett received his early training, which made it possible for

The Potteries that Bennett left for the lights of London.

him to obtain employment with a firm of solicitors in London.

In the Bennett family, the sexes were equally divided - three sons and three daughters - and Arnold was the eldest. Both Arnold and his father knew the anatomy of the Pottery towns thoroughly, and I never tired of exploring them under their guidance. I gleaned from them interesting details of the remarkable growth of many of the factories; some of them huge concerns, which had been raised from very modest beginnings. They cited instances of enterprising workmen setting up 'Potter's wheels' in the rooms of small dwelling houses, and gradually expanding till they became factories of great proportions, employing vast numbers of workpeople. The numerous pottery kilns (or ovens as they are called locally) all vomiting smoke of varying density, in the course of time have besmirched the churches, public buildings and domestic architecture with grime, giving them all a very sombre and melancholy appearance. This prevailing grime evidently made a deep impression on Bennett in his youthful days, for he often remarked on it after he settled in London, and has repeatedly referred to it in his writings.

4. LOCAL ATTACHMENT

In some respcts we can read Marriott's remarks as those of a real-life counterpart of Mr Loring, the fictional outsider of Bennett's short story 'The Death of Simon Fuge'. Loring is a British Museum curator, not a resident of the Five Towns, and his initial reaction to encountering the industrial grime of provincial life expresses in condensed form the sense of Bennett's early hostility to his home town:

> It was squalid ugliness, but it was squalid ugliness on a scale so vast and overpowering that it became sublime. Great furnaces gleamed red in the twilight, and their fires were reflected in horrible black canals; processions of heavy vapour drifted in all directions across the sky, over what acres of mean and miserable brown architecture! The air was alive with the most extraordinary, weird, gigantic sounds. I do not think the Five Towns will ever be described: Dante lived too soon.[26]

It was those early years spent in the company of Marriott's family, and artistic circle of friends which dramatically modified Bennett's view of the

Potteries and of beauty, its perception, definition and representation in art
- all key theoretical issues lying behind the composition of *Anna of the Five
Towns*. An extract from Bennett's 10 October 1897 letter to H.G. Wells gives
some sense of what was happening:

> I am very glad ... to find that the Potteries made such an impression
> on you. I lived there till I was 21, and have been away from it for 9
> years, and only during the last few years have I begun to see its
> possibilities. Particularly this year I have [been] deeply impressed by
> it. It seems to me that there are immense possibilities in the very
> romance of manufacture... not wonders of machinery and that sort of
> stuff - but in the tremendous altercation with nature that is
> continually going on - and in various other matters...
>
> I am sure there is an aspect of these industrial districts which is
> really grandiose, full of dark splendours, and which has been
> absolutely missed by all novelists up to date.[27]

A year later and Bennett was consolidating his ambivalent
relationship with his home town, hinting, in an article for *Black and White*
magazine, at an epiphany that would see him transform the grime of
environmental reality into literary gold:

> The towns are mean and ugly in appearance - sombre, shapeless,
> hard-featured, uncouth; and the vaporous poison of their ovens and
> chimneys has soiled and shrivelled the surrounding greenness on
> Nature till there is no country lane within miles but what presents a
> gaunt travesty of rural charms. Nothing could be more prosaic than
> the aspect of the huddled streets; nothing more seemingly remote
> from romance. Yet romance dwells even here, though unsuspected
> by its very makers - the romance which always attends the alchemic
> of skilled, transmuting labour. The infrequent poet may yield himself
> to its influence as, wandering on the scarred heights above the
> densest of the smoke-wrack, he suddenly comprehends the secret
> significance of the vast, effective Doing which here goes forward...[28]

Bennett will become this poet of the industrial landscape, but first there is
the matter of breaking into print.

5. BEGINNING OF SUCCESS

Towards the end of the first year of Arnold Bennett's residence with us, he entered a competition for a prize of £20 offered by the Editor of "Tit-Bits", for the best humorous condensation of a novel by the then popular writer Grant Allen. The title of the novel has escaped me, but I have a very clear recollection of the pleasurable excitement caused by the news that he had succeeded in winning the prize.

That £20 was the first 'big money' he had earned by his pen, and it led to my suggesting that he should try his hand at writing a novel himself; and in view of his subsequent achievement as a novelist, it seems surprising that he immediately turned down the idea as preposterous. He argued that he had no gifts in that direction, and that his literary interests were in bibliography.

Later on, however, he was persuaded, and he began to devote his spare time to the writing of his first novel, *The Man from the North*, which was published by John Lane in 1898. He wrote this novel in my house, and I still have the bureau at which he sat while writing it; and it is one of my most treasured possessions. In this connection, there is an interesting note published from his journal, in which he says, 'I have never done anything except at the suggestion of my friends. They told me to write a novel, and I wrote one. They told me to write a play, and I wrote one. (Stay! I bought my first yacht entirely on my own initiative, and in defiance of advice.)'

When Arnold Bennett came to live with us, we had only one bureau which was kept in the dining room, and he occasionally used it while writing. He found it both comfortable to sit at, and convenient for keeping his materials together; considerations which determined him to get one of his own. That bureau was the first piece of furniture he purchased in London.

We went out together searching a number of antique furniture shops in Chelsea for one suitable in size and quality, and we eventually found the right article in a shop in the Fulham Road.

When, at the end of six years he decided to rent a house of his own, he sold the bureau to me for the price he had paid for it; but I am afraid it has never been kept so tidily as he always kept it.

He wanted more rooms than we could spare, in order that he could accommodate his young sister and brother, Tertia and Septimus. Tertia was studying singing and Septimus had gained a National Scholarship for Sculpture, tenable at South Kensington.

After considering the possibilities of various houses in various districts, he eventually elected to live at No. 9, Fulham Park Gardens, a house which answered his requirements, and was agreeably situated between Chelsea and Putney where many of his friends lived.

6. PRIZE PARODY

The novel that Marriott cannot recall is Grant Allen's *What's Bred in the Bone* (1891). Bennett used the same title for his prize-winning parody published in *Tit-Bits* on 19 December 1891. He won against formidable opposition from some 20,000 other hopeful entrants. In *The Truth about an Author* (1903) Bennett recognises the vital role played by Marriott's circle in the story's birth:

> It happened that the most popular of all popular weeklies had recently given a prize of a thousand pounds for a sensational serial. When the serial had run its course, the editor offered another prize of twenty guineas for the best humorous condensation of it in two thousand words. I thought I might try for that, but I feared that my friends would not consider it 'art.' I was mistaken. They pointed out that caricature was a perfectly legitimate form of art, often leading to much original beauty, and they urged me to enter the lists. They read the novel in order the better to enjoy the caricature of it, and when, after six evenings' labour, my work was done, they fiercely exulted in it. Out of the fullness of technical ignorance they predicted with certainty that I should win the prize.[29]

I have written elsewhere, in my 'Introduction' to *Lord Dover & Other Lost Stories*, of how Bennett was 'evidently concerned still in 1913 to protect his hard-won literary reputation by emphasising that his circle of artistic Chelsea friends saw no inconsistency between caricature and aesthetic value'.[30] Readers today might have difficulty in discerning much of 'original beauty', and recoil at the casual contemporary, but now offensive, reference to 'sugary niggery'. That caveat apart, I contend that Bennett's parody 'reproduces the plot and that imitates the style, tone and sentiments of Grant Allen's original serial with impressive accuracy, together with an impressive ability to maintain a fast farcical pace which disintegrates into incoherence'.[31]

WHAT'S BRED IN THE BONE.
A CONDENSATION IN SIX PORTIONS OF MR.GRANT ALLEN'S £1,000 PRIZE NOVEL.

I.-A CAUTION TO SNAKES.

Once upon a time a pony was carrying a young lady to the railway station. If that pony hadn't jibbed you would never have experienced this happy moment.

But it did, and the young lady nearly missed the train. If she had, the world would have lost a great book (and, we must also add, a most diverting condensation thereof). But she didn't. A porter managed to insert her sylph-like form in a second-class carriage just as the train commenced its mad career, and she found herself "alone-with an artist."

Thus, at the very beginning, the hero and heroine were brought together, Cyril Waring and Elma Clifford.

Cyril was an artist (an admirable trait in a hero). Elma was the daughter of Mr. Reginald Clifford, C.M.G., a man who had written his name in his country's history as governor of some comical little speck of a sugary niggery West Indian Island. Description of her is useless. Heroines always baffle it.

Briefly, she was charming-and dark. Cyril and Elma were together, but there was no one to introduce them. The course of true love never did run smooth.

However, Elma betrayed a natural anxiety to sit down, and it happened that Cyril was travelling with a snake of considerable magnitude, which he was putting into a picture. She was on the point of converting this snake into a pulp, when Cyril, apologizing for its presence, snatched the animal from a fearful fate. They began to talk, and in a few minutes a keen ear might have caught the whistle of Cupid's arrows in that carriage.

She knew at once that he was an artist. Not by his raiment (for he was not arrayed like one of these), but by her woman's intuition. She had that badly.

The same reader will also note that Elma immediately became chummy with the snake.

They chattered on. He half offended her, and she was about to stand on her dignity, when the train rushed into a tunnel. There was a low, dull thud, and a quick blank stoppage, and Elma found herself deposited in Cyril's arms.

The clever reader has foreseen a collision, no doubt. Ah! Well, it just wasn't a collision. No! the tunnel had fallen in. Cyril and Elma extricated themselves from the remains of the carriage, and attempted to run back. But fate frowned, and the tunnel gave way in the rear of the train also. They were locked in.

II.-NOT QUITE SIAMESE.

From the darkness of the tunnel Cyril and Elma came out, not in weekly parts, as might have been expected, but complete in two volumes.

They were rescued after being buried alive for fifteen hours. Elma's father called it incarceration.

In his manly bosom and her tender breast love smouldered, and they knew it not.

They met again, at a garden party. The opportunities for a tête-à-tête were not so frequent and free as at their last interview, yet they managed to suck romance from a glance, a blush, a smile, a squeeze of the hand.

Now Cyril was one of twins. The other was Guy. And the physiology of these twain was so similar that they had the toothache together.

But whether or no they used the same soap is not recorded.

The problem, which was most like the other, was a life-study to many. And the origin of the twins, even as the origin of sausage, was veiled in mystery and doubt. None knew it, save one.

At the garden party, where Cyril and Elma learned to love, was Colonel Kelmscott, of Tilgate.

The Colonel, upon being suddenly introduced to Guy, was, appropriately enough, knocked into a cocked hat. He thought he had covered his emotion, but he knew not that Elma and her mother were afflicted with hereditary intuition, which is the worst sort.

The fact was, and we state it without reserve, that the Colonel himself was the origin of the twins.

III.-NIGHT THOUGHTS.

On the night of the horticultural gathering, as Elma sat in her bedroom, thinking upon the Manly Bosom, she felt herself gradually seized by a power which compelled her to arise and make a violent excursion around the room, whirling and dancing. What the power was she could not describe. She thought she was mad.

But it was not so. She was merely the descendant of gipsy snake-charmers. The polite said that she had Roumanian blood.

It came to the same thing.

When, after this, the Manly Bosom, bursting with love, proposed for her hand,

Elma spoke to him kindly but firmly. The reason of her refusal she kept secret.

Of course the explanation was that she was too conscientious to become the wife of the husband of a lunatic. Now Cyril thought that her objection related to himself.

On the night previously referred to, the origin of the twins had a worse time of it even than Elma. Snakes and boas certainly consist chiefly of tail, but they have no entail. The Colonel enjoyed an entail, and it simply played Hamlet with his night's sleep. The sight of the twins had awakened remorse in this way.

Before his present marriage he had, in strictest privacy, tied the knot with a poor girl who died in becoming the mother of the twins. Disguised as a gay bachelor, he then, under the paternal orders, walked off with the affections of the Lady Emily, who was his second wife. The fruit of this second venture was Granville Kelmscott, who was brought up as the heir of the entail, a rôle which he adorned.

The peculiarity of an entail is that it will break but not bend. The Colonel decided to break it. Without descending to unnecessary family details he informed Granville of his intentions.

That young gentleman was astute enough to guess that the Colonel had known family cares for a longer period than he had been led to believe.

He had secretly exchanged hearts with Gwendoline, daughter of Gilbert Gildersleeve, Q.C.

As a younger son, he could not ask her to carry things to the bitter end. He vaguely told her that all was over, and set sail for the Cape.

IV.- OUR FRIEND THE ENEMY.

Now the twins had a friend who stuck closer than court plaster, and he lent lustre to the name of Nevitt. He was a bank clerk and a villain. They knew he was the former.

And when he had assimilated £6,000 of their money they knew he was the latter; but not till then. Which was an indiscretion, and showed lack of insight.

He speculated. And his capital was large, for he traded on Guy's innocence. Naturally, he put Guy in the way of making his fortune.

But the company went the way of other companies, and the liquidator stood to win £3,000 each from Guy and Nevitt in the way of calls. And neither of them had such a thing about him.

Now, we must tell you that the Origin, in order to get a night's sleep, had anonymously placed £6,ooo to the credit of Cyril at his bank, and the twins knew not who had done this thing. Cyril was away on the Continent, and Nevitt induced Guy to write out a cheque in his brother's name for this amount. It was merely a matter of convenience, he said, and could be explained afterwards.

Ordinary people call it forgery; but, then, ordinary people are so atrociously prosaic.

Nevitt took charge of the money (he was ever kind), paid his own calls, and proceeded to put himself into another county. He wanted a change of air.

It was here that he met Gilbert Gildersleeve, Q.C., aforementioned. The barrister was strong and fat - much fatter than a certain skeleton which he kept in his cupboard. He thought Nevitt was trying to get a private view of this skeleton. Words ruled high in the market, and they so far forgot themselves as to come to blows.

The Q.C. had large hands, and he, quite unintentionally, choked the bank clerk. End of Nevitt. And thus he got his change of air.

V. - AFRIC'S CORAL STRAND.

When Guy realised that he had been relieved of that £6,000 he developed a healthy appetite for Nevitt's gore, and went after him. Entirely ignorant of his late friend's sudden exit from a weary world, he managed to get himself suspected of the murder.

He heard that the hearts of the police ached for one fond look at his face, and, thinking only of the forgery, he decided that South Africa was the best place for him.

On board the steamer he met Granville Kelmscott. They were half-brothers and knew it not, but before they returned they were half brothers and knew it.

Cyril was arrested for the crime. On such occasions it is highly inconvenient to be exactly like someone else who is wanted.

Gildersleeve offered himself for the defence, and being in truth a great criminal barrister, he won his case. Elma attended the trial, and it had been better for Gildersleeve if she had never been born. During the hearing she had a severe attack of intuition.

She looked at Gildersleeve, and from that hour he never had a moment's happiness, although shortly afterwards he was promoted to the Bench.

She knew who was the murderer of Montague Nevitt.

And he knew that she knew.

And she knew that he knew that she knew.

VI.- KNOTS CUT AND TIED.

Time passed on - it seems to be about all he is capable of doing - and Guy and Granville had adventures in South Africa. They startled the natives, and the natives startled them. It was a new and strange kind of business.

But they made it pay, which is everything.

And they came back, heralded by cablegrams, and Granville found peace in the arms of Gwendoline Gildersleeve.

Guy intended to give himself up for forgery, but the police weren't having any. They said that murder was about his size, and Guy felt doubly injured.

The great Sir Gilbert Gildersleeve presided at the trial. He was pale, and we don't blame him.

When the jury returned a verdict of "Guilty", Judge Gildersleeve arrived at the conclusion that he was in one of the smallest-sized corners ever constructed.

After all, he wasn't a bad sort. He told the jury that he was sorry to disagree with them, but he himself had assisted at the despatch of Nevitt to another clime.

He continued to behave sensibly and died.

Cyril, now that he could marry without making his wife the sister-in-law of a supposed murderer was anxious to join the charming descendant of snake-charmers in an attempt to solve the problem whether marriage really was a failure.

Moreover, the Origin had expired, and he enjoyed great riches.

And Elma had discovered from a relative that her terpsichorean and boa-constrictor tendencies were not a form of madness, and would gradually wither to their primeval atoms.

And so they lived happy ever afterwards.

At least, we suppose so.

****

I was not aware of any subsequent use of 'What's Bred in the Bone' as either a novel or a short story title. Not, that is, until the great Canadian writer Robertson Davies chose it for his 1985 novel, for which he chose the epigraph '"What's bred in the bone will not out of the flesh": English proverb from the Latin, 1290'. This intricately plotted novel is almost as frenetic and filled with bizarre events as Bennett's parody.

But there is another reason for my pursuing this proverbial reference down what might appear to be a labyrinthine dead-end, since it provides me with an opportunity to remark on Davies's great admiration for Bennett. In *Conversations with Robertson Davies*, he lauds Bennett as 'an extremely fine writer' whose 'The Old Wives' Tale is, I think, is one of the most remarkable novels of this [20th] century'.[32] A comment from one master novelist to another I consider well worth a brief critical detour.

7. CHARACTERISTICS

Arnold Bennett had a number of profoundly individual and striking characteristics, which provided the caricaturists with very easy and useful material. His wayward front lock of hair. His slightly protruding irregular front teeth. His corrugated chin and full drooping eyelids. Even the peculiar way he walked was a distinguishing individual feature that marked him out from his fellows.

Then there was the marked impediment in his speech which was distinctive and individual too, and I think it was a source of worry to him. He didn't actually stutter; for he would never allow himself to do that, but he would wait varying lengths of time until he could pronounce the word he wanted. The pause periods were embarrassing both to himself and his listeners. He once said that with an effort he could overcome it, but that it was rather exhausting.

He made no special exertion when talking to his most intimate friends; consequently his impediment was worse at such times. At first I ventured to prompt with the word I thought had escaped him, but he did not like it, and with emphasis he said, 'Frederick, never attempt to help me in that way'. The admonition was entirely effective, and from that day I was always a patient listener. As is usual in such cases, he showed no signs of the impediment when he was singing, or when talking to children. He loved little children, and instantly won their affection, and he behaved like a big care-free boy in their company. He was 'Uncle Arnold' to a large number of children who were in no way related to him.

It is curious, that in spite of the many years Arnold Bennett lived in London, and the lengthy periods he spent in Paris and other places on the Continent, he never lost certain North Staffordshire characteristics, and there was always a noticeable flavour of his native county in his accent.

Although he was one of the most generous, warm-hearted, and kindly of men, he steeled himself against showing any sign of emotion under any circumstances whatever, which gave a false impression, and caused some, who didn't know him intimately, to think his nature rather hard at times.

He was unfailingly helpful to all young authors, artists and musicians who appealed to him for assistance or advice, and there are many who owe a large measure of their success to his timely help.

His home training, and the exacting requirements of his early work in solicitors' offices, developed his natural love of tidiness until it became an obsession, and it must be included in the list of his characteristics. His writing table was at all times an object lesson in tidiness.

Punctuality was another of his characteristics, and he disliked unpunctuality in others, and resented it. I never knew him to be late for an appointment, or to arrive too early, and I often wondered how he always managed to appear exactly to time. I have an ardour for punctuality myself, but I could never compete with his abiding accuracy.

Shortly after he went to live in Cadogan Square Chelsea, I received a letter from him, asking me to go to breakfast, to meet a mutual friend who was there on a short visit. The time he gave was eight o'clock. I arrived a little before the time, and sat in the waiting room reading the morning paper. Bennett came in exactly at eight, and producing his watch said 'I'm not late'. I said 'No, I was ten minutes too early'. Of course, the breakfast was ready to time, and of course, the visitor came down a quarter of an hour late, a fact that was playfully brought to his notice.

Bennett claimed never to have missed a train, and yet, by his studied calm, and never-in-a-hurry demeanour, he often gave the impression that he would do so. My restless anxiety on such occasions used to amuse him, and once when I started away without him, feeling certain he wasn't allowing sufficient time, he came sauntering up the station platform, and stepped into the compartment of the train, which I had been waiting in for ten minutes, just as the guard was waving his flag for it to start.

8. A TRIO OF WRITERS

Throughout his lifetime, Bennett's friends paid tribute to his unfailing generosity to family and to friends in need, and to his efforts, often behind the scenes, to helping writers in creative, financial or legal difficulties. As Marriott says, he 'was unfailingly helpful to all young authors, artists and musicians'.

One young author who benefited greatly from Bennett's avuncular creative encouragement was the South African writer Pauline Smith (1882-1959). They first met by chance in December 1908 in the Hotel Belvedere, Switzerland, where Pauline was staying with her widowed mother; Bennett, there with his wife Marguerite, was writing his comic novel *The Card*. Martin Laux summarizes their initial meeting thus:

> Mrs Smith recognised Mr Jacob Tonson (one of Bennett's pseudonyms) and introduced herself to him. Mrs Smith told Bennett that Pauline wrote. Bennett spoke with Pauline and persuaded her to let him read everything she had written. Bennett subsequently invited her to tea with him and Marguerite, and provided feedback. Bennett considered the Scottish stories could have been written by anyone, but the South African sketches [of her homeland] had great potential. ...With encouragement Pauline started writing a new story...[33]

That 'story' eventually became her first published collection of short stories, *The Little Karoo*, in 1925.

In her charming memoir *Arnold Bennett ...'a minor marginal note'* (1933), Smith pays tribute to Bennett as her devoted friend and mentor throughout the rest of his life. Remembering that first fateful meeting she writes:

> In all our wanderings I had remained inexperienced in life, and in literature. I knew myself to be ill-read. Of all these short-comings I was painfully aware, and in company the shyness and self-consciousness they caused made me awkward and silent. Yet in spite of this, because I too wrote a little, A.B.'s interest in me as a fellow-craftsman was at once aroused... A.B., sitting reading near by, heard the hubbub [caused by my poor bridge play], and as it subsided pushed towards me with a smile a torn scrap of the margin of his newspaper [hence the sub-title of the memoir] on which he had written: 'I know why you play badly. You are thinking of something you are trying to write.

> Such was his first greeting to me as a fellow-craftsman... later he asked to see, and in spite of my alarmed protests insisted upon seeing, all the little I had written since leaving school.[34]

Over an invitation to tea Bennett was unsparingly critical of Smith's early work while still having the generosity of spirit to tell her that she showed great potential and had the makings of an artist.

> No one had ever before called me an 'artist', and though I could not believe myself to be one, there was something within me which knew how bad my novel was and leapt to the justice of his verdict. His damning of those opening chapters gave me a confidence in his

judgement which no praise could have won, and brought me so overwhelming a sense of relief and release that it was as if he had broken down for me an imprisoning wall and drawn me out into the open air.... And I made a friend whose honesty and sympathy, patience and understanding, were never to fail me.[35]

Such was the bond of pupil/master friendship between them that after Bennett's death in 1931 Smith found it impossible to complete the novel she had been working on: 'for - as a friend who provided constant encouragement - he might have chivvied her out of her increasing self-doubt, her growing despair at European fascism and its implications for a racially defined South Africa, and even her chronic ill-health, which she sometimes felt was exacerbated by her failure to write'.[36]

Bennett had a very different, and distant, relationship with D.H. Lawrence. Despite Lawrence's prickly nature where he perceived charity was involved, Bennett was at the forefront not only in defending *The Rainbow* from the censor, but more materially in coming to the younger writer's monetary aid. At one point in 1918 Lawrence's financial affairs grew so desperate that he told J.B. Pinker, his and Bennett's literary agent, that 'I am afraid in another fortnight I shall not have a penny to buy bread and margarine'.[37] He also wrote to Pinker suggesting Bennett as a possible benefactor: 'I am sorry to tell you that I am coming to the last of all my resources, as far as money goes. Do you think that Arnold Bennett or somebody like that, who is quite rich out of literature would give me something to get along with'.[38] When Bennett was confidentially shown the letter his response, despite his own pressing financial demands, was immediate: 'I would willingly subscribe something towards a regular fund for Lawrence, say £1 a week for at least a year, if you think this would help and if you could get other subscriptions.'[39] In the event support from other writers was lacking, leaving Bennett to privately donate £25. On this, and other occasions, Bennett saw no reason why his generosity should be made known to the recipients.

Over the course of his career Bennett never wavered in his public support of writers whose work he thought was unfairly under attack from censorship, whether from Church, State, or influential public figures. One of his last such campaigns was in support of an unknown young female novelist, Norah James, whose 1929 novel, *Sleeveless Errand*, had attracted the censors attention for so-called use of obscene language.

Bennett launched a spirited defence of the book in his *Evening Standard* 'Books and Persons' column, expressly appreciating Jones's use of the vernacular: '...it records realistically the chatter of a familiar type of person who cannot express themselves at any time on any subject without employing words beginning with "b"'.[40] Bennett's intervention failed to prevent the novel being banned, but when it was published by the Obelisk Press in Paris in 1929 its dust-jacket came lauded with quotations from his article. When Bennett and James met in Lamorna, Cornwall, in the summer of 1930, the young novelist took pleasure in being able to personally thank him.

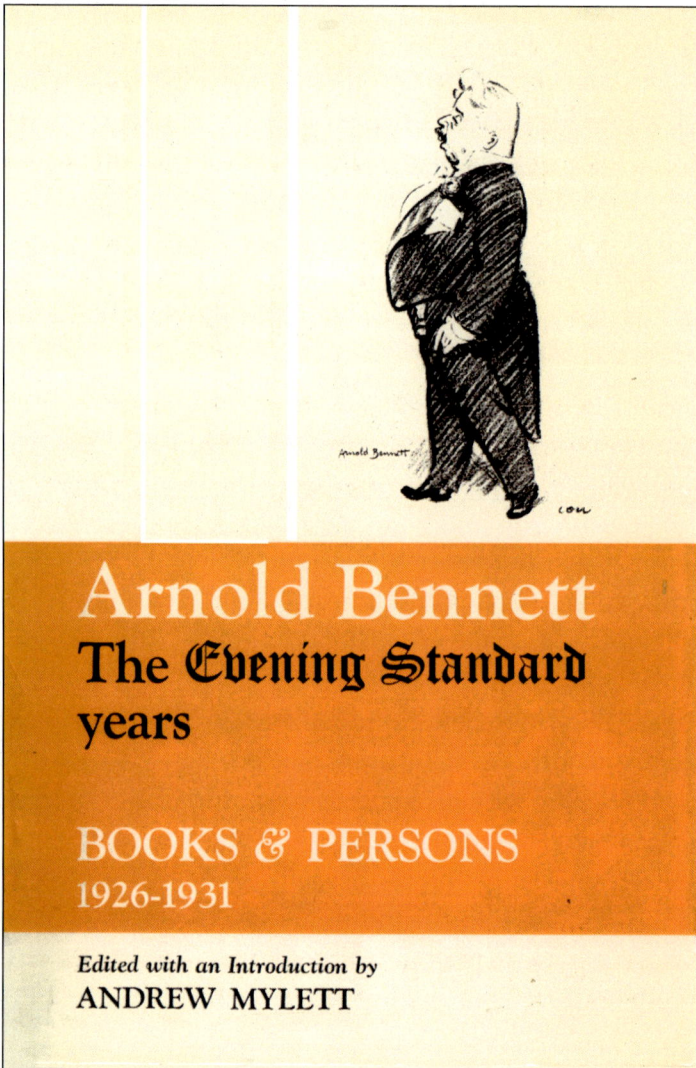

Arnold Bennett
The Evening Standard years

BOOKS & PERSONS
1926-1931

Edited with an Introduction by
ANDREW MYLETT

9. CYCLING

Cycling was another interest which Arnold Bennett and I had in common, for it was at this time that it developed into the most popular of sports. It became a craze; and every grade of society was 'bitten' by it.

Groups of 'smart' people daily indulged in the pleasure of riding round and round the various London Parks, and Society cyclists could be seen taking breakfast in Kensington Gardens and Battersea Park after their morning run.

It was the introduction of the 'safety' bicycle that was responsible for this phenomenon, for it made it possible for women as well as men to ride. No woman had been sufficiently daring to mount into the saddle of the old Penny Farthing type of bicycle, with its sixty inch front wheel; but when the specially designed bicycle for women was put upon the market, myriads of the fair sex were immediately attracted to the sport.

Of our group, Fred Alcock was the pioneer, and under his advice and persuasion, Bennett, Sharpe, and I became possessed of bicycles, and shortly afterwards Mrs. Sharpe and my wife took cycling lessons, and used to join in our excursions into the country.

Arnold Bennett was a strong rider, and he took up the sport with his characteristic thoroughness, and in common with the rest of us, looked upon it as a delightful way of solving the ever present problem of exercise in the cause of health.

It is very pleasant to recall the many week-end runs we had to Kingston, Ripley, St. Albans, Windsor, Pangbourne and many other interesting places within easy reach of London.

I remember that we affected the road-racing type of machine with the low curly handle-bar, for which we had to suffer the penalty of stiff necks and aching backs at the end of the long journeys. But we preferred to sacrifice our comfort rather than give the impression that we were mere fledglings at the game.

We all joined the Cyclist's Touring Club, and proudly flaunted the Club badge, and always claimed the prescribed rebate from our Hotel bills which our membership entitled us to. The club membership was a distinct advantage when touring, and secured for us preferential treatment at most of the Hotels on the club list.

One Saturday afternoon when Bennett, Alcock, Sharpe and myself had cycled down to Pangbourne, where we arrived at sundown; while we were having dinner it was arranged that we should start on the return journey immediately after breakfast on the following morning. I then declared my intention of getting up at 5.30 a.m., and exploring the little town before leaving.

The other members of the party were agreed on the folly of such an enterprise, but all their arguments failed in turning me from my purpose; but having failed in argument, they concocted a more effective method of checking my early rising propensities.

I rose promptly on time next morning, only to make the disconcerting discovery that my trousers had disappeared. I was helpless, and there was nothing for me to do but crawl ignominiously defeated back into bed again, and wait patiently for my nether garments to be restored to me.

It was not until my watch registered nine o'clock that they were delivered to my room with the shaving water

My entry into the breakfast room was the signal for much merriment, and the conspirators were mockingly clamorous for my impressions of the picturesque spots of Pangbourne at sunrise, and asked to see my sketches.

The success of this practical joke served my friends with material for banter at my expense for a very long time.

In those days, when I used to go sketching round the outskirts of London, Arnold Bennett often cycled with me, and would lie on the grass with a book while I was sketching, and when I happened to do a sketch which pleased him, he would make me a sporting offer for it.

One evening he came into my studio while I was studying a map of the East coast, in search of a good sketching ground for the summer holidays. 1 had decided to make a tour on my bicycle and investigate that portion of the coast lying between Felixstowe and Southwold. I briefly outlined my scheme, and to my delight he said he would go with me, and we settled to make an extended week-end of it.

On the following Friday morning we loaded up our cycle-carriers with necessities for the journey, and in order to avoid being delayed by the congested traffic in the East-end of London we went by train as far as Romford.

It was easy cycling along the mildly undulating Essex roads to Colchester, and we were in great form for our evening meal, and after a quiet jaunt in the town, we put up for the night.

Next morning we encountered a strong head wind which rather

distressed us, and the nineteen miles to Ipswich tired us. However, after a good lunch and a short rest, we felt better, and we walked about until tea time in the hope that the wind would either turn, or soften down before we moved on to Felixstowe, our next objective.

But by this time the sky was heavy with clouds ominously suggestive of rain, and the wind had still further freshened to gale force, and we debated whether we should go by train to Felixstowe; but unwisely, as it turned out, we decided to carry on by cycle. We had only gone two or three miles, when large spots of rain began to fall, and we took shelter under some road-side trees, while we put on our mackintoshes.

As soon as the storm abated a little, we pushed on with difficulty against the wind, which made the going slow, and we still had about twenty miles to go.

It commenced to pour with rain again, but we came to the conclusion that if we spent any more time sheltering, we shouldn't be able to complete the journey to Felixstowe that night. But before we had covered a dozen miles, we were forced to take shelter, for it was impossible to make much headway against the blinding rain, which was coursing down our mackintoshes into our shoes.

After a time, the violence of the storm slackened, and the wind eased down, so we rode on in the steady rain, (which seemed to be on for an unlimited run,) feeling anything but comfortable.

It was rapidly getting dark, and to add to our discomfort, we were ill-advised by a farm labourer to take what he called 'a short cut' when we were within three or four miles of the town.

The short cut turned out to be a tortuous unlighted road, very rough and muddy, and incised with deep waggon-wheel ruts which took much longer to negotiate than if we had kept to the main road. After what seemed an incredibly long time, the lights of Felixstowe came into view, shining through a curtain of rain.

We found the streets deserted and the houses in darkness, save for occasional lights to be seen in upper-room windows; indicating that the inhabitants had retired for the night.

At the first Hotel we came to which bore the gilded badge of the Cyclist's Touring Club we drew up, and when we dismounted, water oozed from our shoes at each step we took.

After repeated knockings, the door bolts were noisily drawn, and a dishevelled heavy-eyed waiter appeared looking anything but pleased at being disturbed. However, our saturated condition moved him to compassion, and we prevailed upon him to provide us with food and liquid refreshment. Further; when we had changed into night attire, he took charge of our wet clothing, which was served to us warm and dry next morning.

That night, two notoriously poor sleepers, slept soundly and well, and were thus compensated for our inclement weather experiences of the previous day.

After breakfast we inspected the features of the town, and found it wanting in pictorial possibilities. It was a quite ordinary sea-side town, and not at all the kind of place I was in search of, so we mounted our cycles again and pushed on to Southwold; glancing at the intermediate sea-side places as we went.

We decided that Southwold and the neighbouring village of Walberswick gave the best indication of good sketching material; and the surrounding landscape was good; so I engaged suitable accommodation at Walberswick.

The expedition resulted in my spending six very enjoyable and profitable weeks in that district, and Arnold Bennett came for a week-end towards the end of the time, as did also my friend James Clark the painter.

10. FREE-WHEELING

Marriott and Bennett were typical enthusiasts for the cycling craze that seemed to intoxicate so many in the Britain of the 1890s, not least women, for whom it opened up literal roads to personal freedom. Given Bennett's many cycling expeditions it is perhaps surprising that the bicycle hardly features in his fiction, other than peripherally as in *The Old Wives' Tale*. It was left to his great friend H.G. Wells to claim the title of writer-laureate of the new cult with the publication in 1906 of *The Wheels of Chance*. Reading Bennett's *Journals*, Wells could well have had Bennett in mind when remarking that the 'cycle is one of the greatest blessings which the nineteenth century has brought us. Its value is simply inestimable to nervous men, and I think all writers are more or less trouble with their nerves ... All the cobwebs are brushed away from the brain, and return to your work really refreshed.' [41]

Marriott's mention of the Cyclists Touring Club refers to the oldest cycling club in the world, founded in Harrogate in 1878. Initially known as the Bicycle Touring Club, it changed its name to include tricyclists in its ranks. The 'gilded badge' on hotels was a guarantee of good accommodation and service for cyclists. Bennett kept a detailed record of hotels visited across Europe and in the U.S.A., and the trip with Marriott and friends to Ipswich was no exception:

> To-night we 'lie' at the Great White Horse, Pickwick's Inn, and by good fortune we have been allotted the Pickwick bedroom, No.36, an immense apartment, accommodating three, and labelled outside 'Pickwick'. On the walls an extremely bad oil painting of a Pickwick banquet. 'A facsimile of this hotel was erected at the World's Fair, Chicago, as one of the celebrated old inns of this country.' In many ways it has been modernized, but still it keeps the air of the ancient hostelry.[42]

Bennett's *Journal* paints a similar grim account of the ride to Ipswich as that recollected years later by Marriott. It reads as a testament to Bennett's sense of deep 'satisfaction of facing and overcoming difficulties, of slowly achieving a desired end, in spite of obstacles':

> Soon after 9.30 it was quite dark, the rain was coming down steadily, the wind ... had increased, and we were riding warily across a wild, naked country on a road of which the narrow cart-ruts formed the only rideable surface; all else was loose sand, sticky and dangerous with rain.
>
> For miles we rode on hardened strips of the road scarcely a foot wide, the wheels of the bicycles continually grating amongst sand and pebbles as we groped our way forward. The rain gradually penetrated our clothing and settled in our shoes, till my feet at least were stone cold. At every few yards we started a rabbit or a stoat or some unrecognizable creature of the night. There were no houses or cultivated ground till we passed through a village only two miles from Felixstowe. After this we lost our way ... My lamp went out, and on dismounting I found that my invalid right arm was useless, and so we walked the last mile to a hotel in the pouring rain.
>
> Marriott vowed that he enjoyed the ride thoroughly. I was anxious, uncomfortable in my saddle, and nervous. Clearly my nerves had not yet recovered from my accident in March. I imagined every possible sort of accident, in each case following out a train of circumstances to the direst possible climax. In particular I dreaded a puncture, and that I might take a cold, to be followed by rheumatic fever.[43]

The cycling accident Bennett refers to occurred only three months earlier

Colchester Cycling Club, c.1898.

on 21 March: 'Dislocation of the elbow. Chloroform operation 22 Mch. I carried my arm in a sling for six weeks. For three weeks I dictated all articles and letters. The orderliness of my existence was never so deranged before. Since the middle of March neither of my books now in progress has been touched'.[44]

Bennett's determination to get back in the saddle as soon as possible is testament to his strong strength of will - but as Marriott's next chapter shows, there were good social and recreational reasons for keeping mobile.

Leek Socialists' Cycling Club in 1898 - one of three cycling clubs in the Town.

11. WITLEY

Following on the rapid growth of cycling as a popular means of locomotion for getting into the country, came the lure of the country cottage, and it became the fashion for town workers engaged in sedentary occupations to rent country cottages for week-end use. Bennett was always to be found among the pioneers of any new movement, and he was quick to adopt this new and amusing form of recreation, and for a year or two he shared a charming old half timber cottage at Witley in Surrey, which was given the playful title of the 'Fowl Hatch', and had at one time been occupied by Madame Sarah Grand the novelist.

The first thing Bennett did was to hire a piano, in order that he could have as many of his musician friends there as the cottage would accommodate. The regular contributors to the programmes of the fortnightly London musical evenings were invited in relays, so there was no shortage of music during his tenancy.

The cottage had no bathroom, but there was a plentiful supply of water from a pump in the back yard, and courageous guests who wished to bathe, could do so by sitting under the pump, while someone else worked the handle. Those alfresco baths were very jolly and boisterous affairs, and added greatly to the gaiety of the week-end holidays.

At that time Stanley Hazell had a song entitled, "The Maiden with the Downcast Eye" of which the first verse ran as follows:

I know a little maiden who is very very shy (Be careful of the girl who's shy)
She has a modest manner and a downcast eye (Be careful of the downcast eye)
She wears upon her forehead a little baby curl, (Be careful of the little baby curl)
And everyone will tell you she's a simple little girl (Be careful of the simple little girl)
There are all sorts of girls, there are many kinds of girls.
Some of them are frivolous and some of them are shy.
You can trust them all no doubt, but you may as well lookout
For the simple little maiden with the downcast eye.

After Hazell had spent a weekend with Bennett at Witley he added the following verse:

If you're staying down at Witley and you want to have a bath,
(Be careful if you want a bath)
You saunter from your bedroom to the sunny garden path,
(Be careful of the nobbly gravel path)
The regulation costume is a blanket and your boots,
(Be careful of the woolly rug and boots)
You take your seat beneath the pump, and then the water shoots,
(Be careful when the water shoots.)
There are all kinds of baths, there are warm and swimming baths,
But the shower bath à la Bennett is the one you all should try though,
as reckless of the weather, He affects the altogether.
You had better pass the 'Fowl Hatch' with a 'Downcast Eye.'

At the next musical evening in my studio, this song was Hazell's surprise item.

12. THE FOWL HOUSE

Bennett had published his first novel, *A Man from the North*, in February 1898. This was set largely in London, but by September he began to seriously contemplate leaving the capital for a rural retreat which he thought would provide the peace and quiet necessary to complete the novel he had been planning since February 1896 or earlier. *Anna of the Five Towns* was eventually published in September 1902, having been completed in a somewhat different rural setting from that of Witley.   Thus in his *Journal* entry for 12 September 1898 we find Bennett deciding 'very seriously to aim at living in the country to the entire abandonment of London. A year ago I could not have contemplated the idea of leaving London, but I have developed since then.'[45] In retrospect Bennett's dream of a rural writer's idyll was never going to work for a man whose very consciousness was infused with the culture of cosmopolitan constructs. But it took four years - years in which family tragedies must have played their part - for Bennett to finally realize the futility of any such permanent relocation. Meanwhile, his 17 September 1898 *Journal* entry shows him pursuing the dream:

Young [publisher of Bennett's early books] and Kennerley [future brother-in-law] and I rode from Farnham to Witley to inspect the house which Young and I are to rent for the next three years. About four centuries old, this house for the last hundred years had been called The

Fowl House, until it was named by its present occupants Godspeace. These occupants are four; C.E. Dawson, a young artist; Morris, a journalist who writes on the connection between Whitman and architecture; Gertrude Dix, the novelist, and Esther Wood, a writer on art ... They are vegetarians and teetotallers - and they wear sandals. They have an air of living the higher life.[46]

A day later and:

Last night I dreamt that I wore sandals and was ashamed. Since seeing the house at Witley I have been quite depressed in anticipation of the time which must elapse before I can leave London permanently for the country. It is as though the next year or two in London will be unbearable.[47]

There is clearly some sort of mental turmoil bubbling beneath the surface of these journal entries from a man who opens his first, semi-autobiographical, novel by asserting that 'There grows in the North Country a certain kind of youth of whom it may be said that he is born to be a Londoner' but cannot help but close the chapter with a self-defeating 'her heel is all to ready to crush the coward and hesitant; and her victims, once underfoot, do not often rise again'. Bennett was never a man to reach for sandals to complete his sartorial elegance and the rural landscape is conspicuously missing

Arnold Bennett at the Fowl House, also known as 'Godspeace', in 1907.

I have only ever seen this photograph reproduced in Reginald Pound's *The Strand Magazine: 1891-1950*.[52] And the Fowl House itself makes but a single fleeting appearance in Bennett's fiction, in his long short-story, 'The Woman Who Stole Everything', set many years later than when Bennett and friends stayed there:

'The telegram said: "Address till Tuesday, The Fowl Hatch House, Stoke Mandeville. Cynthia Smythe"'[53]

from his fiction. And when he did move out of London for these four years he took its values with him, never losing contact with its vibrant social and cultural life. Perhaps Witley, and later Trinity Hall Farm in Hockcliffe, rural Bedfordshire, provided just that mental and geographical distance from city/town life to allow Bennett to write his first great novel of life in the Five Towns.

Surprisingly, Bennett's published letters and journals nowhere mention the previous illustrious female writer inhabitant of the Fowl House, identified by Marriott -- Sarah Grand. Such an omission surprises me because Bennett had interviewed her at her London home at some length for an article in *Woman* magazine, 2 May 1894. Even more pertinent, several of his early published stories, beginning with 'The Heavenly Twins on the Revolt of the Daughters', published in *The Westminster Gazette* (10 February, 1894), refer to Grand's 1893 novel, *The Heavenly Twins*. I have included all these stories in my edited volume *Arnold Bennett's Uncollected Short Stories, 1892-1932*,[48] and explained in the 'Introduction' the hostile reception for Grand's novel as deemed to be dangerous and perverting with its uncensored portrayal of female venereal diseases caught unsuspected from wayward husbands. To add further to some contemporary readers' consternation there was a cross-dressing heroine who was determined to escape the late-Victorian constraints of her sex. Bennett, however, saw it as making a 'a fearful breach in the walls of the Home ... The book was eagerly and gratefully accepted by women, who perceived in it not only the bold utterance of their timid aspirations, but also a distant hope of release from the somewhat Ottoman codes of men'.[49] This quotation comes from Bennett's extended essay on Sarah Grand included in his 1901 collection, *Fame and Fiction: An Enquiry into Certain Popularities*, in which he judges *The Heavenly Twins* 'the modern equivalent of *Uncle Tom's Cabin*'.[50]

Bennett's *Woman* interview with Grand remains one of the first, if not *the* first, examples of the celebrity interview nowadays so familiar to readers of Sunday Supplements and gossip magazines. Its pioneering journalistic status has gone unremarked, in part because, along with Bennett's own subsequent silence, there has to date been no critical examination of Bennett's early journalism, which includes important assessments of a range of late-Victorian writers across many genres. Its appearance in this book marks a significant re-discovery of a forgotten aspect of Bennett's early literary career:

A Chat with Mme. Sarah Grand

Considering that I am a man, and but an average one, I felt flattered when Mme. Sarah Grand asked me to look in and have tea and a chat with her. I must confess, however, that when I arrived at the door of the house which contains her little Kensington flat, and saw written in bold type in the entrance hall the name of her whose doctrines had been discussed in hushed whispers, the sense of self-congratulation for a moment gave way to a feeling of timidity.

But it was too late to turn back. I pulled myself together, ascended and knocked, and a moment later was awaiting my hostess in a pretty little blue and white drawing room. Her greeting re-assured me, and Mme. Grand, who I had until then seen only in evening dress - which in a woman is often deceptive, although it sometimes conceals but little - bore none of the outward signs of feminine aggressiveness.

However, I thought it wiser to stick to common everyday subjects, as I have always been nervous in the presence of a woman with a mission. So I began with the weather, and then was about to begin with the first line of the conventional conversational formula of the moment by asking my hostess whether she had read The Heavenly Twins, when I realised just in time that this question - the great stand-by of stranded conversationalists of to-day - would, under the peculiar circumstances, be a little out of place. Having missed the first link, I failed to get the second. Dodo ought to have come to my rescue; but I could not for the life of me, recall the name of Mr. Benson's 'boom-book'. And to make matters worse, there had been no bomb outrage for several days, and I had not seen the new play of the previous week. Thus I happily recalled a paragraph I had just read in that evening's Globe which referred to Madame Grand, with no particular object beyond that of ventilating two terrible puns upon her book and her name, which the writer had presumably been treasuring up in one of the pigeon-holes of his mental store cupboard. I referred to it with many apologies for the profession of journalism, and we wondered why such things were written, and whether or not the County Council could interfere; and thus we got to the subject of the Press in general, and of her critics in particular.

'Nothing annoys me more,' said Mme. Grand, 'than the mistake made by so many in supposing that I took Colonel Colquhoun as a typical man. Only last night at a dinner party Mr. ......'(naming a well-known literary character) - told me how mistaken I was in supposing that my principal male character was a fair type of the sex. Of course I only meant him to be typical of a particular type - not of the whole sex.'

'And you do not think us very bad I asked?' I asked, feeling more at ease.

'Oh! Dear no. I am far from being a man-hater, I like and respect many men.

Moreover, there is not, and never can be, any quarrel between the sexes. Women will always be women, and men always men, and marriage, in my opinion, must always be the ideal state.'

'But you do not sympathise with the bachelor girl?'

'Yes, certainly. I do not think any worse of a woman because she won't run the risks of matrimony. The glorified spinster distinctly interests me.'

'And your ideal married life?'

'That there should be absolute equality between the two, but not on the same lines; each in his or her own sphere, and that if there is to be a head it should be the husband. Personally, I should most admire a husband whom I could show deference, whom I could consult on every subject. It would be such a pleasant, lazy, irresponsible existence, but it would not be quite ideal from a wider point of view.'

'And you think a woman should be domesticated?' I asked, prepared for another surprise.

'Absolutely. That is her line. I myself, busy as I am, know all the details of my ménage. I love domesticity, and sometimes long to throw down my pen and take up a piece of plain needlework'. (Mrs. Grand's tea, at any rate, was excellent, and I wondered whether a housewife's character could be judged by tea as by handwriting.)

'Then you do not believe in emancipation?' I asked, more surprised, and certainly more at my ease than ever.

'Not in the hackneyed use of the expression; not in the emancipation of women from womanliness and natural ties of wedlock, but certainly in emancipation from shallowness and ignorance.'

'And a woman's dress?'

'Should be suitable to the sex and the occasion. I cannot bear to see a woman lounging on a London drawing-room sofa in what is little less than a Highland shooting costume, any more than I should admire a woman riding in the Row in a teagown. Affected masculinity in dress seems to me foolish, because inappropriate and uncomfortable.'

'I presume you have made many enemies in consequence of your book?'

'Many more friends than enemies. For instance, I am quite surprised myself at the number of clergymen who have written expressing their appreciation of The Twins. The way in which the book was received by the Press affords an interesting study. Papers representing the very young school of affected culture, or those which I believe unconsciously reflect the private characters of journalistic Don Juans, attacked me furiously in the most bitter manner, but gave me good advertisement hereby. Other papers showed extreme caution, combined with faint

praise. The Daily Telegraph was, I think, the first important paper that "discovered" my book and foresaw its success.'

'I suppose you have a very extensive correspondence?'

'Yes, very. In fact there is no end to it. Fortunately one of my stepsons is at home now, and acts as my secretary, and his post is no sinecure. I get letters from "sincere admirers" who want to borrow sums varying from £5 to £50, on the ground that they have failed while I have succeeded. I receive poems, too, from ladies who are sure they are born to win fame by their poetry, "if only they can get a start", and ask my opinion of worse than commonplace verses; and one lady threatened to commit suicide if I did not get her poetry published very soon.'

'Is it published?'

'I am afraid not; but I think she is still hopeful. It is very sad, this curious phase of life that one sees in the letters that I suppose are received by everyone who has made more or less of a name.'

And so on to subjects that savoured less of "shop", until when I rose to leave, I had realised that there was nothing unwomanly - quite the reverse - about the author of The Heavenly Twins.

****

A year after Bennett's 'chat' appeared, Jane T. Stoddart published an 'Illustrated Interview: Sarah Grand' in the magazine *Woman at Home*. This makes for a fascinating companion piece to Bennett's earlier interview, containing a series of photographs of Grand's apartment, including both the entrance hall and the drawing-room referred to by Bennett. Stoddart's interview also reproduces a number of portraits all carefully selected to suggest multiple facets of Grand's personality and artistic credentials. Interestingly, the portrait that shows 'a dreamy nature sensitive to art and beauty, yet governed by a strong purpose'[51] is similar to a portrait reproduced alongside Bennett's interview, and is credited to the same photographer, namely, H.S. Mendelssohn.

What I find particularly uncanny about this chapter of Marriott's memoir is the discovery of a thread unravelling over nearly 50 years, from the 1890s, when Bennett and his friends rented Fowl House, to 1939 when the National Register entry records Marriott occupying a modest bungalow less than half a mile down the main road - Petworth Road --from the Fowl House. Incidentally, the Fowl House was impressively renamed The Lion's Gate some 30 years ago, a step up the animal hierarchy that might have amused Bennett.

13. EXPERIMENTS IN PICTORIAL EXPRESSION

Soon after Arnold Bennett came to live in Chelsea his inborn love for art became active, and he began to make regular visits to the National Gallery, and the annual exhibitions of the various Art Societies. He kept up this practice all through his life, and there were few important exhibitions he missed seeing.

From the first he was more particularly attracted to the art of water-colour painting, and as time went on he became more and more interested, until he determined to experiment in that medium himself. He procured the necessary equipment and set to work; devoting such time to painting as he could spare from his regular work. This new development resulted in our having many enjoyable hours of out-door sketching together, and the excursions we made on our cycles in search of subjects constituted some of the chief joys of our long association.

Many of them occurred in the country around Fontainebleau, and though many years have passed since the Fontainebleau days, they survive as some of the most delightful of memories.

It was in that part of France, while staying with Arnold Bennett and his wife, that I got my first introductions to the fascinating charm of the old-world towns, and the beauties of the French landscape; and I have since made many enjoyable tours in that picturesque country in search of subjects for painting and etching.

It was during one of those early cycling excursions with Bennett that I received my first vivid impressions of historic French chateaux, which inspired me to make a long series of studies of those fine romantic buildings. He expressed the opinion that the French, as a people, had more reverence for their castles and ancient buildings than we have for ours in England, and he applauded their care of the fabric. Certainly there are many instances in France, where the draw-bridges over the moats are kept in perfect working order, but perhaps they carry the restoration of the buildings too far; giving the impression at first sight, of their being comparatively new, and making them dependent on their architectural features and guide books for an indication of their great age.

I was astonished at the rapidity of Bennett's progress in sketching; the more, because of the limited time he was able to devote to it. His skill in drawing and his sense of proportion and colour values, combined with the rare ability for analysing form, were quite remarkable. Moreover, his trained powers of observation served him well in the selection of his subjects; with the result that his paintings were well composed; for successful composition commences with, and is dependent upon, careful selection of the material.

In view of his capabilities as a draughtsman, I tried to persuade him to do some studies in the methods of Girtin and other masters of the British school of water-colour painters; by first drawing the subject carefully in outline with a pen or fine brush, and then applying washes of colour. He didn't favour the idea, because it did not admit of his completing his sketch at one sitting, which was always his aim.

In recent years there has been a revival of the firm out-line method of procedure, and the tinted drawing has become increasingly popular among water-colour painters, particularly with those who devote a good portion of their time to etching. I regret that he never experimented with the outline method, for I am convinced that it would have suited him admirably.

His method was to work right away in full colour over a slight drawing. No torturing of the paper by scrubbing and sponging, or scraping out lights with a knife, but simple directness, careful selection, and an emphasis of essentials.

I firmly believe that if Arnold Bennett had elected to adopt art as his profession, he would have made a name either as a painter or etcher, and would have brought a newness of vision, combined with a frankness of expression, which would have enriched those arts. He possessed marked natural gifts, and whatever pictorial subject-he engaged upon, he treated in a spirited and spontaneous manner.

His facility with the pencil, and the direct and expressive character of his line impressed me at once, and the unerring force of his draughtsmanship caused me to suggest that he should experiment in etching and dry-point on copper. The idea interested him, and he soon took it up, and while the enthusiasm and the opportunity of indulging it lasted, he produced quite a number of plates. He was obliged to confine his work to the 'dry-point' process, because the elaborate equipment necessary for true etching, and the time absorbed in preparing the plates with wax grounds; treating them in the acid bath, 'stopping out' the various stages of the work with varnish, and the subsequent re-grounding and 're-biting' of the plates, made it impracticable.

RESTORED TEXT

For the benefit of those who are unacquainted with the process of Dry-Point I will opine a brief description of it. Although it is often used in combination with etching, strictly speaking it is not etching, because it doesn't require the use of an acid. It is a dry process.

A dry-point is produced by drawing on a highly polished copper plate with a sharp pointed steel needle, or with a diamond point. The steel point, sharpened to a more acute angle than for etching, is used for deeply incised lines, and the diamond point is generally employed for fine lines. Under varying degrees of pressure, the point cuts into the surface of the copper, making a furrow with a turned up edge, technically called 'burr'. The burr, when new, holds more ink, and has a more velvety and richer printing capacity than an etched line, but it is very fragile, and wears away quickly in the process of printing; consequently fewer first quality impressions are obtainable from dry-points than from true etchings. The progress of the work can be seen by rubbing printing ink into the lines, and smartly wiping it off with the palm of the hand.

It is the added richness given to the line by the burr that is the chief distinguishing feature between a dry-point and an etching, so that when the dry-point tool is used in conjunction with etching, the burr is scraped away to bring it into harmony with the etched work.

When the subject is completed, proofs are taken by covering the plate with thick printing ink which is screed from a 'dabbler', and then wiping the plate fairly clean with printer's muslin, and afterwards with the palm of the hand. A piece of damped paper is then placed over the plate, and then it is passed through the printing press under great pressure. The print is then carefully lifted from the plate and pinned on to board to straighten it and dry.

Of all the varied forms of artistic expression, none are capable of providing greater thrills or disappointments than etching or dry-point. Each plate is an adventure, however skilled the artist may be, and the pulling of a first proof is invariably fraught with exciting moments.

****

Arnold Bennett was severely critical of his efforts to portray in water colours the emotions which the ever changing beauties of nature aroused in him, and he invariably came away from the subject he had been sketching lamenting the imperfections of his achievement; but occasionally, when reviewing the work next morning, he would find consolation in the discovery that after all it possessed merit.

14. PAINTING FOR PLEASURE

Whilst it is undoubtedly the case that Bennett took seriously to watercolours as a result of his friendship with Marriott and friends, there were early signs that his talents were not to be restricted to the written word. His Aunt Bourne's child-hood gift of a box of watercolour paints was to be the start of a lifelong love affair with painting and sketching. Not that his childhood enthusiasm was always matched by an ability to convey image to paper. That he nevertheless persevered was due to the embarrassment and humiliation endured as an eleven year old schoolboy hearing his poem on the topic of Courage being ridiculed by his classmates: '... I can recall no further interest to write a story for at least ten years ... I forthwith abandoned fiction and went mad on water-colours.'[54] Bennett's amusing initial assessment of his artistic ability in *The Truth about an Author* finds a later echo in Marriott's remembering him 'lamenting the imperfections of his achievements':

> The insanity of water-colours must have continued for many years. I say insanity, because I can plainly perceive now that I had not the slightest genuine aptitude for graphic art. I never got beyond the stage known technically as "third-grade freehand", and even in that my "lining-in" was considered to be a little worse than mediocre. O floral forms, how laboriously I deprived you of the grace of your Hellenic conventions! As for the "round" and the "antique", as for pigments, these mysteries were with-held from me by South Kensington. It was at home, drawn by a futile but imperious fascination, that I practised them, and water-colours in particular. I never went to nature; I had not the skill ... I was content to copy. I wasted the substance of uncles and aunts in a complicated and imposing apparatus of easels, mahlsticks, boards, Whatman, camel-hair, and labelled tubes.... Every replica that I produced was the history of a disillusion. With what a sanguine sweep I laid on the first broad washes - the pure blue of water, the misty rose of sun-steeped places, the translucent sapphires of Venetian and Spanish skies! And then what a horrible muddying ensued, what a fading-away of magic and defloriation of hopes, as in detail after detail the picture gradually lost tone and clarity.[55]

Bennett was always his own strictest critic, but his technique was surely not as disastrous as he would have readers believe, since in

Bennett's Landermere watercolour,
one of his illustrations for Cyril Ionides and J.B.Atkins: *A Floating Home.* [57]

October 1884 he was awarded the prize of *Easy Studies in Watercolor* from his home-town's Wedgwood Institute for his art composition, 'Sound, Light and Heat'. And notwithstanding the prize book's title, Bennett rarely took things easy, becoming in time an accomplished amateur water-colourist and sketcher, always ready to take advice.

Bennett's 9 September 1913 *Journal* entry offers a near perfect miniature portrait of what he would consider a typical well-spent pre-War day, including an afternoon in Marriott's company searching for picturesque landscape settings. It gives a vivid sense of a man at the height of his powers, ready to follow his own self-help advice on how to live on 24 hours a day:

Yesterday was a proper sort of day for my trade. 400 words before breakfast. After breakfast, newspapers, cigar. Then 800 words. Then dictation of letters. A few Muller [keep-fit] exercises. A quarter of an hour in garden. A section of Lavisse's *Histoire Gênêrale.* Lunch. Flaubert's correspondence. Sleep. Early tea. In car with Marriott to Landermere to make a watercolour - 4 to 6 o'clock. Car came back to fetch our things. We walked home. Over two miles, mostly uphill and over rough ground, in 29 minutes. Profuse perspiration. Change. Bath. Dinner. Champagne. Cigar. Coffee. Bed at 10 P.M. and a very fairish night. Absolutely no time at all cut to waste between 7A.M. and 7.30P.M., when we dine. I can always do more work when I have many other things on hand, and when I am following a programme that is rather a tight fit for the day.[56]

And to conclude this chapter on a further positive note, Bennett already at this time held the early rare distinction amongst his literary contemporaries of seeing one of his paintings gracing the American dust-jacket of his own novel, *Carlotta* (1905).[58]

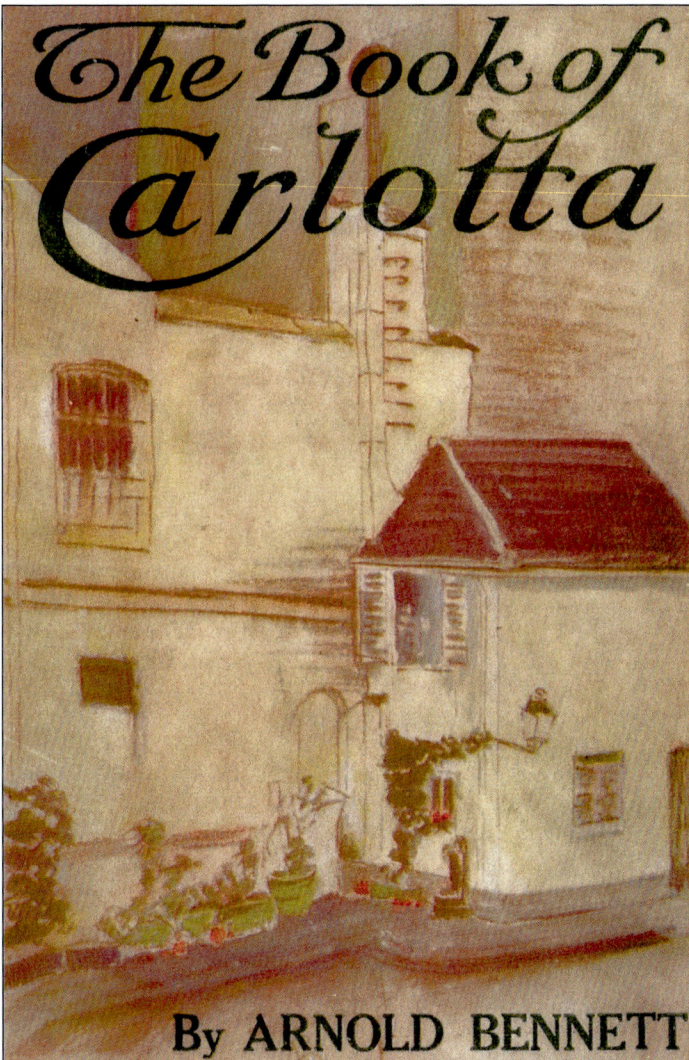

The Book of Carlotta

By ARNOLD BENNETT

15. WESTMINSTER CATHEDRAL

A frequent visitor to the house in the days when Arnold Bennett was living with us, was E.A. Rickards, a brilliant young architect, (a member of the firm of Lanchester Stewart and Rickards) and we both gained a lot of valuable information on architectural matters in the course of our long friendship with him.

Rickards was profoundly interested in his profession, and vehemently extolled it as the greatest of all the arts. He never tired of talking architecture, but his talks were invariably punctuated with strong language, deploring the apathy of artists, and the public generally towards architecture. This idea constantly obsessed him despite the fact that he, and those associated with him, had been eminently successful in securing many important commissions in open competition. Notable examples being the Cardiff Municipal Buildings, the Deptford Town Hall, and the Central Hall, Westminster, which stands on the site of the old 'Aquarium'.

One day Rickards came along and suggested that the three of us should go and see the new Westminster Catholic Cathedral, which was then in course of construction. We immediately fell in with the idea, and as all agreed that we were suffering from the lack of exercise we decided to walk to it. It was our habit at that time to attribute all our ailments to the want of exercise. The route we chose was by way of the Chelsea embankment and along Queen's Road, past the Chelsea Pensioners' Hospital, to Buckingham Palace Road and Victoria. As we walked, Rickards, who was in one of his pessimistic moods, treated us to one of his passionate outbursts against things in general and the architectural position in particular. However, as soon as we entered the Cathedral all his pessimism immediately melted, and for the moment he forgot the pet theme he had been so forcefully elaborating, and he broke into an enthusiastic appreciation of the genius of Bentley, the architect of the building.

As we threaded our way among the disordered mixture of building implements and materials, we were profoundly impressed by the spaciousness of the interior, with its vast areas of unpointed and undecorated brick work. Fortunately, Rickards knew the clerk of the works, so we were free to roam about the great building at will.

I have never seen Bennett more intensely affected than he was by that great imposing architectural skeleton, unfurnished by surface decoration, and he questioned whether it would ever look finer than it did then, in its crude rugged grandeur.

But a more thrilling experience followed, when we mounted to the top of the great tower. It was a very difficult ascent, made by climbing ladder after ladder to the various landing stages, which were constructed of loosely laid planks across the scaffoldings. There were no hand-rails round the platforms, and it was the more exciting because the ladders were strictly vertical.

This was the first of a number of visits made by Arnold Bennett to the cathedral while it was in process of building, and in one of his writings he has given a graphic account of his seeing the solitary figure of the architect Bentley, walking about inside the building at dusk; well knowing that he would never see the crowning work of his life completed; for he was stricken with the deadly disease of cancer! A more pathetic and arresting spectacle it would be difficult to conceive, and when he related the incident to us, we judged that he had been deeply moved by it.

Arnold Bennett always took a great interest in architecture, and this interest was nurtured by his carefully chosen architect friends and his many travels abroad, and he had a sympathetic eye for the best productions in very divergent styles. While he had a respectful regard for tradition, he never allowed it to intimidate him, and he was quick to recognize merit in the newest and even revolutionary methods in architectural construction and presentation.

16. THE ROLL-CALL

Bennett's keen interest both in pictorial expression and in architecture spilled over into a strongly worded objection to the cover art and layout for his 1918 novel, *The Roll-Call*, which I have critiqued elsewhere as the 'twentieth-century's most considered Anglo-American appreciation of the role of the architect in society'.[59] When reading Bennett's letter to his literary agent, J.B. Pinker, we should remember that it comes from an author who from the out-set of his career was conscious of the aesthetic appearance and appeal of books as objects of art in their own right/write:

> I have received some copies of *The Roll Call*. They are odious in a very high degree. I do not complain of the quality of the [war-time] paper ... I object more strongly to the illustrated cover being passed without reference to the author and still more strongly to the descriptive

matter not being submitted to the author. The description of the book inside the jacket: 'Can a man love two women is the theme of this book' is perfectly ridiculous and extremely misleading. Really Hutchinsons ought to have more sense than to make fools of themselves and of me in this style.

The cover is merely painful.[60]

Perhaps not surprisingly *The Roll-Call* was the only one of Bennett's books that Hutchinsons published. And Bennett surely had a point. From the opening sentences of the novel, architecture takes centre stage: 'In the pupils' room of the offices of Lucas & Enwright, architects, Russell Square, Bloomsbury, George Edwin Cannon, an articled pupil, leaned over a large drawing-board ...'.[61] Whereas the cover art does indeed privilege notions of romantic estrangement over background hints of architectural concerns, there is also a nice irony in Bennett setting the firm's office in the heart of Virginia Woolf's Bloomsbury in a text that uses built space to reveal his characters' inner psychological complexity.

The character of George Edwin Cannon in *The Roll-Call* is very much based on that of Edwin Alfred Rickards (1872-1920). Bennett and he met at one of Marriott's musical evenings in the early 1890s, remaining close friends from that moment on. Bennett contributed 'A Personal Sketch' to what turned out to be a posthumous study of *The Art of E.A. Rickards* (1920) in which he married admiration for his professional life with amusing personal anecdotes:

> I do not exaggerate when I assert that none of his friends would call him a tremendous optimist, nor when I assert that he did not live about half a century without discovering grievances against the universe. As I write this I have an ancient vision of Rickards, in the old days when bicycles first had free-wheels, practising the free-wheeled bicycle for the first time in front of my house in France. Unquestionably Rickards got off the bicycle with a distinct grievance against the inventor of that disconcerting contrivance the free-wheel. Unquestionably he had an idea, confused but powerful, that the inventor of the free-wheel had invented the free-wheel for the special purpose of disconcerting just him, Rickards. The episode, trifling enough, furnished a good instance of the exercise of the acute critical faculty which Rickards could always bring into play upon the men and things constituting his environment. [62]

Whatever his idiosyncrasies, Bennett thought that 'Rickards always had a zest for life and for all the manifestations of life, such as I have seldom seen equalled and never surpassed'.[63]

As Marriott writes, it was thanks to Rickards's esteem for the architect John Francis Bentley (1839-1902) that the three friends made frequent visits to Westminster Cathedral, over the course of which Bennett's youthful enthusiasm for architecture was reawakened. His *Journal* entry for 22 May, 1901 marks the point at which the idea for *The Roll-Call* began to germinate:

> Rickards and I, in the evening, went over the vast, unfinished Roman Catholic Cathedral in Victoria Street, and found it distinguished, impressive, a work of great and monumental art. Bentley, the architect, was wandering under the dome, examining and enjoying his mighty production; the realization of a conception which must live for many centuries. It was an impressive sight to see him, an impressive thought to think that one has seen him so, this magnificent artist, who started life as a stonemason, and is now slowly dying of cancer of the tongue. He wore a frock-coat and silk hat, but a necktie of black silk tied in a loose bow.[64]

This experience made a deep impression on Bennett, resurfacing 17 years later to set the tone for *The Roll-Call,* with architecture as the love of George Cannon's life, not the 'two women' of the dust-jacket blurb:

> Suddenly, out of Victoria Street, they came up against the vast form of the Byzantine cathedral.... The gate in the hoarding that screened the west front was open. With a large gesture he tipped the watchman a shilling, and they passed in like princes. The transition to the calm and dusty interior was instantaneous and almost overwhelming. Immense without, the cathedral seemed still more immense within. On one side of the nave was a steam-engine; on the other some sort of mill; and everywhere lay in large heaps the wild litter of construction, among which moved here and there little parties of approved pygmies engaged silently and industrially on sub-contracts; the main army of labourers had gone. The walls rose massively clear out of the white-powdered confusion into arches and high domes; and the floor of the choir, and a loftier floor beyond that, also rose clear. Perspectives ended in shadow and were illimitable, while the afternoon light through the stone grille of the western

windows made luminous spaces in the gloom.[65]

Then, just as earlier recorded in the *Journal*, they spot a solitary figure in a frock-coat and a silk hat 'gazing around in the dying light':

> George literally trembled. He literally gave a sob. The vision of Bentley within his masterpiece, of Bentley whom [his employer] worshipped, was too much for him.... Bentley, beginning life as an artisan, had succeeded supremely. And here he stood on the throne of his triumph. Genius would not be denied. Beauty would conquer despite everything. What completed the unbearable grandeur of the scene was that Bentley had cancer of the tongue, and was sentenced to death. [66]

Architecture, its practitioners, and their built spaces, occupy the foreground of *The Roll-Call*, but they are also a constant presence in many of Bennett's essays, journalism, and non-fiction writing. Bennett's tour of the United States in October 1911, for example, allowed him to enthuse over the modernity of New York's skyscrapers whilst also appreciating Washington's architectural homage to European tradition:

> ... the Capital appeals to the historic sense just as much as any other vast legislative palace of the world - and perhaps more intimately than some. The sequence of its endless corridors and innumerable chambers, each associated with event or tradition, begets awe. I think it was in the rich Senatorial reception room that I first caught myself being surprised that the heavy gilded and marmoreal sumptuosity of the decorations recalled the average European palace.[67]

By way of contrast, Bennett's time at the Front as a war correspondent between 21 June and 15 October 1915 resulted in a very different lament for the destruction of France's architectural heritage. His series of magazine articles appeared in book form as *Over There: War Scenes on the Western Front* in which there is a lingering impression that Bennett regrets the destruction of buildings as on a par with the loss of human life. Every one of the book's included seven on-site sketches by Walter Hales illustrates the destruction of the material world wrought by artillery bombardment. There is the sense that whilst human life may continue, historical structures are irredeemably lost: 'The Town Hall (like the Cathedral here and at Rheims) had no military interest or value, but it was the finest thing in Aras, the most loved thing, an irreplaceable thing'.[68]

17. MUSICAL EVENINGS

While I was studying at South Kensington, I used to attend some of the concerts given by the students of the Royal College of Music, and I was fortunate in forming a friendship with two of the students there: Herbert F . Sharpe, a brilliant young pianist, and J. Cliffe Forrester, an organist and composer. Our close friendship survived the student period and was maintained after we were all launched in our professions, and furthermore, had married and become responsible citizens and house-holders.

Herbert Sharpe inaugurated a system of weekly musical evenings which were held alternately at our respective houses, and at the house of our mutual friend and medical adviser Dr. J. Farrar; who came from the same Yorkshire town as Sharpe, and who had a practice in Putney.

Thus it came about, that when Bennett took up his abode with us, he found a musical fraternity established after his own heart, and he immediately brought his enthusiasm for music to bear on these gatherings with his accustomed thoroughness.

The evenings were divided into two parts, the first being devoted to classical music. After a short interval for refreshment, the second half was given up to a sort of variety entertainment which afforded any amateur members of the audience an opportunity of contributing. For this part of the performances there was no set programme, the members being called upon to play or sing just anything they felt inclined to do, or tell any of the funny stories then in circulation. This casual hap-hazard method didn't fit in with Bennett's temperament, and he at once set about to bring order out of the chaotic system he found existing. The go-as-you-please programmes weren't good enough for him, and offended his methodical sense of management.

First he began by writing out the programmes on sheets of note paper, from which I was deputed to announce the items. Afterwards they developed into leaflets with decorated covers which I designed. As time went on, these evenings became increasingly popular, and the audiences grew in numbers until an average attendance of between thirty and forty was reached.

Previous to Arnold Bennett's management, there had been no kind of record kept of the number of these entertainments, but he was careful to keep a complete set of the programmes which were all numbered; so when the hundredth musical evening approached, it was made the occasion for a special effort. Extra invitations were issued which resulted in my studio being filled to capacity.

Bennett's faculty for organisation was allowed full play, and the evening proved to be a memorable one, and ranked as a considerable achievement. The date was the 20th April, 1901, and it was the first and only occasion when a machine printed programme was used at any of these evenings.

When the 'General Entertainment by the Entire Company' part of the programme was reached, Bennett gave his first performance in London of a light humorous song he had learnt in his school days, entitled 'Sucking Cider through a Straw'. The only portion of it I am able to remember is the chorus, which ran, 'With cheek to cheek, and jaw to jaw. Both sat sucking cider through a straw a-aw - a-aw - a-aw'. It was a very popular item, and came as a surprise; for no one present excepting his relatives knew that he could sing.

With the exception of Macaulay's 'The Armada', all the items in the second part were specially written and composed for the occasion. The 'Impromptu for Piano' ascribed to Paderewski was nothing more than spoof from beginning to end.

Stanley Hazell who had an extensive repertoire of humorous songs was the principal performer in the second half of all the musical evenings, and always before he commenced to sing, the position of the piano had to be changed, in order that he could face the audience without too much strain being put upon the muscles of his neck. Very occasionally he had a difficulty in remembering the words, and at times a part of the accompaniment would escape him, but he always managed to turn the temporary lapse into fun, which really enriched the entertainment. One of these episodes provided Bennett with the theme for a parody of Sullivan's famous song of 'The Lost Chord', which I had to sing as a burlesque of the self-satisfied mannerisms of the professional tenor, the Drawing Room darling of that period.

The Lost Song, or Hazell's Fix

I

Seated one night at the piano,
When the music was done
And the supper was won
And the fun had begun
And the moment had come
For my share of the show.
I was planted there to warble
A song I did not know.
I quite forgot what the words were,
And what the theme was then;
But I vamped one vamp like a vampire
In the style of Beet-ho-ven.
Like the sound of
A Sonata
Waldstein, Gluckstein
Moonlight, Nightlight
Passionata
Trio, Brio
Symphonic
Pastorale
And Chorale,
By "By -By -Beet -ho -ven."

II

It wandered off to the skylight
And do what I would
Though I tried all I could
And the keys they shed blood
It swore that it should
Not return from on high.
Then it changed to the Irish Christening
With a touch of the down cast eye,
It went into modulations
Like Bach over-coming Brahms
And wore the harmonious blacksmith
Into Purcell's patent Psalms.

It linked both the choir and the table
Into opus a hundred and eleven
And trembled away into silence
As though it had got to heaven.

III

I sought but I sought it vainly
That comic song divine
Which stuck in the soul of the piano
And would not enter mine.
It may be a whiskey and soda
Will teach me that song again.
It may be that only cocoa
Will ease me of my pain;
It may be that no refreshment
Will help me my song to find -
It may be that only at the thousandth
(spoken) musical evening
I shall call its strain to mind.

Arnold Bennett, 1901

Many parodies of popular songs were written for the 'Variety' parts of these musical evenings by Bennett, Hazell, and Alcock. A very amusing parody of Tosti's song 'Goodbye Summer' was written by Alcock, under the title 'Draw Nigh Plumber', and for my imitation of the mannerisms of a High Church Parson, Bennett wrote Chronicles in Biblical style, founded on the skating-rink craze which was prevalent just then:

CHRONICLES OF OLYMPIA

"Dearly Beloved, here beginneth the sixteenth chapter of the *Chronicles of Olympia*, the first and following verses.

Now it came to pass, when Imrie, who was also called Kiralfy and the Greatest-on-Earth, had passed away from, the land with all his host and laden with spoils, that a rink was spread abroad beneath the roof of Olympia.

And a certain young man of the tribe of Isaacs, whose name was Solomon, arose within his house on the seventh day at even, and begirt himself in fine raiment, saying, I will go forth to my beloved, but first I will call on the brother of my father.

Now Solomon Isaacs in the days of his youth had been one of them that sell tidings in the street at nightfall, and he was among the knowing ones of the world.

And as his strength grew with years, so his guile increased, and he waxed fat without labour and rich without toil, for behold he promoted certain companies which are called limited.

But the day of his misfortune came, and a man of exceeding great authority, yea, even the liquidator came unto Solomon Isaacs, and said unto him, Solomon, disgorge.

And Solomon disgorged.

Therefore in the time of his adversity, it became a law unto Solomon that he should visit the tent of his father's brother. And upon this night also went he to the tent of his father's brother, bearing certain jewels.

And he said unto his father's brother, Uncle, how much? and his father's brother answered and said. Two shillings, and a ticket.

Then went Solomon to the house of his beloved, and knocked, and called, Eliza, Eliza, Eliza, even to the third time.

And she heard, and ran out to him and kissed him within the gate.

And he said unto her. Thy breath is as the scent of sweet aloes, tinctured with onions of Spain. Hast thou any left?

And she answered. Yea, and steak also. Enter my beloved, and eat thereof. And he did so.

And when he could carry no more, he said unto her, Eliza, wilt thou even go with me to the great rink of Olympia? And Eliza prepared an exceeding bland smile, which spread to the uttermost parts of her countenance, and the width thereof was two cubits, and the height thereof was two cubits.

And she said unto him. What thinkest thou?

And Eliza arrayed herself in the colours of the rainbow, and set two feathers of an ostrich upon her head, and upon her feet stockings white as snow-long-fallen. And her face was like the red rose and the yellow rose, but her neck was dark even as the shadow of a cloud of Lebanon, and her ears were a sombre mystery which none have solved. And behold her circumference was goodly, and her years were as the sands of the sea. But of these she spake to no man.

And it came to pass when they arrived at Olympia, that a man sat beneath the lintel at the receipt of custom.

And Solomon Isaacs reasoned with the man that he should abate his charges, but the man would not. Then was Solomon wroth, for he was poor but dishonest.

Now when they came to the Inner Court, they beheld many young men and maidens gliding hither and thither upon wheels. And Eliza spake to her beloved and said, Beloved, we will go and do likewise, and he answered, yea; and joy was upon his forehead.

And they planted themselves firmly upon the wheels even upon the little wheels, and said unto the slave which stood by, In what manner set we out upon our journey? We would fain more, but lo, we are glued to the ground. And the slave said. Strike out boldly and trust in heaven. And Solomon whispered to his beloved, saying, A Firmament is in mine eyes. And she said, The back of my head swelleth like new bread in a child's stomach. And divers men in the vicinity uttered words of wickedness, calling upon them to arise and make room, but they could not.

Then the slave who had set them upon the wheels ran forward, and lifted them up quickly, for he had lifted up many.And they set forth like the lion of the forest, creeping upon its prey.

And Solomon said, Eliza, Eliza, take heed. I exult not in pain and I have no comfort. The sweat standeth on my brow, and my paths drop fatness.

But she answered lightly. What is my strength that I should wait? And what is my end that 1 should be patient?

Then said Solomon, Is my strength the strength of stones?Or is my flesh of brass? Is it not enough that I have no help in me, and that effectual working is driven quite from me?

Yet a little space went they on. Their track was the track of the drunkard at midnight, and their feet made excursions of their own accord.

And lo, Solomon, being in sore straits, loosened the circumference of his beloved, and she went upon her own way, and when she was afar off she turned round and sped backwards; but she knew not why she did this.

And when Solomon looked again, behold his beloved lay still, and the pillars of the court trembled. Then said Solomon unto himself, The way of the backsliders is hard.

And she cried out to him with a loud voice to go to her. And he went warily, saying. Yea, I have seen the foolish take root. And even as the spider, the great spider, he sat down beside her.

And lo, great multitude fell upon them for those seats were not numbered, neither were they reserved, and in the days of Imrie who was also called Kiralfy and the Greatest on Earth.

Now it came to pass, when the multitude had unpiled itself that a great sickness came upon Eliza, and she spake to Solomon, enquiring gently whether or no he had brought with him a certain lotion.

And he answered, yea verily.

And he placed his hand within his coat, and straightway a great sickness came upon him also.

And he said, Eliza, sorrow hath overtaken us. And she came nigh to weeping, and threw her arms around his breast. And lo! she felt somewhat of dampness oozing through his raiment.

And she lifted up her voice in wailing, saying, Solomon, Solomon, Thawest thou?

And he answered, I thaw.

And it came to pass that their tears mingled with the whiskey which was spilled, and of the broken bottle no man knoweth the fate.

Here endeth the *Chronicles of Olympia*.

Arnold Bennett.

From the time of their inception, these musical evenings were always interesting, but after they came under the efficient directional influence of Arnold Bennett, the character of the programmes improved very much, and developed into thoroughly well organised entertainments which were both instructive and pleasurable. I believe that it was his association with these entertainments that led to his writing the three drawing room farces which were published by his friend Chas. Young of Messrs Lamley & Co. in 1899, under the title of *Polite Farces* .They were designed for presentation in ordinary costume, with ordinary furniture as properties, and one door for entrance and exit.

****

RESTORED TEXT

'IN A PUTNEY GARDEN'. A SONG CYCLE.
WORDS BY STANLEY HAZELL.
MELODIIES BY VARIOUS COMPOSERS.

1. I'll tell you a tale without any plan,
   At Putney there's a famous clan
   Who every fortnight to a man
   Turn up to hear the grand pian-
   O played in a way that nobody can,
   But Herbert Sharpe of Putney.

2. There's Marriott with the raven hair,
   And Ravenshaw has motored there
   And Young and Kennerly I declare,
   And Bennett too, and Jack Farrair,
   Have come from near and far to hear
   The pianist of Putney.

3. Our lady friends we mustn't forget,
   There's Mrs. Marriott you can bet,
   And Mrs. Farrar, Mrs Led-
   Ward, sometimes Tertia Bennett,
   And Mrs. Fat-and-simple Pet,
   And Mrs. Sharpe of Putney.

4. At seven o'clock we make a start,
   Beginning with the serious part,
   And turning to the programme smart
   We find the first is a grand Sonat-
   A, written by the great Mozart,
   And played by Sharpe of Putney.

5. Then Frederick Marriott comes along
   And sings a charming tenor song,
   His upper C delights the throng,
   For Frederick Marriott's going strong
   And so is the giddy accompanying
   As played by Sharpe of Putney

6. At most of the regular gatherings
   We have some very charming things
   Arranged for pianoforte and strings,
   And played by Mrs. Sharpe, who brings
   Her fiddle along to the evenings,
   Got up by Sharpe of Putney.

7. Then Edgar Homan, cheerful lad,
Will keep us from feeling sad
By playing something blithe and glad
Upon his famous Kiddem Strad,
With which he once was badly had
Though not by Sharpe of Putney.

8. And sometimes, more enchanting still
A trio figures in the Bill
And then Tschaikowsky makes us thrill,
As played with superhuman skill
By Tennyson Werg, and Fernie Hill,
And Harold Sharpe of Putney.

9. Whoever else may take the floor
Your always find there's one perfo-
Mer doing the work of half a score,
That most prolific contributor
And punisher of the piano for-
Te, Herbert Sharpe of Putney.

10. He'll play a fugue, an Op.
Of speed he'll go at the very top,
As just as you think he's bound to drop
He'll give his forehead a hasty mop
And go again without a stop,
Will Herbert Sharpe of Putney.

11. When the musical programme is ended
Backs are unbended, and ways are wended
To the room where we all are intended
To partake of a frugal repast.
No further inducement is needing
For proceeding to the feeding.
The ladies as usual are leading
The men follow on and come last.

12. There in the Dining Room
Tables are laden with endless variety.
Lots of lovely things to eat
And plenty of beautiful drink.

Pork pies - pies of pork
Staffordshire pies fit for any Society
Sausage rolls with golden crust
With innards of delicate pink.

13. There are sandwiches too by the plateful
Tittilateful - very grateful.
Even those who find sandwiches hateful
Can manage a dozen of these.
They are none of your stale preparations,
That at stations try out our patience.
But really artistic creations
Of potted meat, salmon and cheese.

14. Plum cake and seedy cake
Pastry galore from the nearest confectioners,
Brown bread and butter and mustard and cress
And biscuits of every kind.
Stewed fruit and fruit in tins
Figs and dates, as good a selection as
As ever I saw of apples and pears,
For beauty and flavour combined.

15. And then to assist locomotion
There's the lotion. Oh! The potion
I'm filled with the deepest emotion
When I think of the liquor drink.
For coffee and tea freshly made is
For the ladies. Oh! the ladies
And for anyone else who afraid is
To let himself go on the wine.

16. Brandy, whiskey, bottles of gin,
Flagons of Burgundy straight from Australia,
Single breasted bottles of Bass
And non-arsenical beer.
Mineral waters by the quart
Made with the orthodox paraphernalia
Hunyadi, Ginger ale
And everything else that'll cheer.

17. And when we have finished our stoking
Oh! The joking, and the smoking.
It really is very provoking
How quickly the time slips along.
So finding the evening is waning
And refraining from complaining
We fill in the time that's remaining
With reading and story and song.

At this stage of the proceedings, there is very frequently a cry for Hazell. And Mr. Hazell, having made his bow to the assembled company, and taken his seat at the second-best piano-forte, proceeds to sing.

1.
The Mary Jane set out from Shields
To sail to a place remote.
2.
And the owl and the Pussycat went to sea
In a beautiful pea-green boat.
3.
Twas the very same day, down Piccadilly way
That I first saw the black creature.
4.
And as Mr. Peter Potter was an awful little rotter,
Mrs Potter took it out of Peter.
5.
And after that in the usual way, In a humorous recitation.
And then if Marriott's feeling gay,
A burlesque imitation,
And then a dialect song by Sharpe,
One of his own composing,
And perhaps a Yorkshire reading too
Before the evening's closing.
6.
It doesn't do him much harm
And does us a power of good,
For the fine old Yorkshire dialect,
So thoroughly understood by us
Is thoroughly understood.

7.

So should you need a little recreation,
And want to hear some music of the best,
You only have to get an invitation
And Sharpe and Co. will always do the rest.
I say without the slightest hesitation,
That nowhere else in London will you find
Such kindly hospitality,
So free from all formality,
As here we have them happily combined.

8.

In good old Putney - that's the place for me,
And Chelsea is included on the motion,
May these evenings never cease,
But continue to increase
In prosperity as boundless as the Ocean.

****

I believe I am right in saying that it was at one of these evenings that Bennett first met Eugene Goossens for whom some years later he wrote the libretto of an opera, *Judith*, which was produced at Covent Garden.

Item No.6 in the programme [of the 100th musical evening] *'Lantern Medley on one Sharpe (with modulations)'* was an amusing lecture on Herbert Sharpe and his friends, specially written for the occasion by Fred Alcock, in which humorous reference was made to many members of the fraternity, and there occurred the following reference to Arnold Bennett:

'I will now pass on to one of Sharpe's most distinguished friends - The Heir of Hockliffe (Slide - Portrait of Bennett). The time Bennett can spare from farming he fills up with authorship, and at one time condescended to edit a well-known journal. We are able to-night to show you a design hitherto unpublished for the title page of this journal which we think will arouse considerable interest.(Slide - a ribald sketch of a girl with the title "Woman-fast but not too forward." Note: The authentic sub-title of the paper was "Forward - but not too fast.) To return to Bennett; we are able to show you a sketch of the burly Bennett and his blear-eyed blood hound Ibsen.

This dog is fed on rejected manuscripts which accounts for his ferocious expression.

These sketches, made by Bennett's friend and admirer, Edwin Alfred Rickards, were courteously placed at our disposal by him. On behalf of Bennett and ourselves we tender him our thanks. We are assured by Mr. Rickards that if he had, himself, drawn the plans for Bennett he would not have made them otherwise.'

A number of the original members of our musical fraternity have passed away, and others have removed to places in the country too remote for them to attend, but the tradition has gone on without a break, and my studio is regularly filled with musical enthusiasts; while famous singers and instrumentalists give ungrudgingly their best art, for the enjoyment of these assemblies.

The generosity of singers and musicians in general is proverbial; but their unfailing liberality with their talents to provide enjoyment to their friends, is a continual source of amazement to me.

In recent years, Arnold Bennett's visits to these evenings were only occasional, but his enthusiasm was as keen as ever, and he was always ready to help young aspirants by giving them letters of introduction to prominent people who were likely to have engagements to offer.

During an interval at one of these evenings, Bennett accepted an invitation to spend a Saturday evening with the Hazells who at that time lived at No. 9, Aylwood Road Forest Hill, and a day or two before the time arranged for his going, he received from Mrs. Hazell full directions as to the best way of getting to their house, together with a cleverly drawn and painted sketch map of the route. This resulted in Bennett composing the following Sonnet in reply.

SONNET

Florence, thou flower so fragrant and so fair,
Thou orchid blooming in a desert place.
Dost think thy loveliness I cannot trace?
For maps and painted plans I have no care.
Wert thou in Timbuctoo or Bloomsbury Square,
I'd find thee. For the radiance of thy face
Shines like a star illuminating space.
And soothes while quickening my divine despair.
But soft! While my fond fancy me absorbs,
I catch the glitter of an angry gaze -

Thy knightly spouse with actuarial orbs
Bids me to tune my lyre to other lays.
Great Scott!.........Yet why indeed should I repine?
On Saturday we meet at Number Nine.

E.A.Bennett.

In view of the fact that Arnold Bennett wrote very little in the way of verse, either serious or light, the above early example is the more interesting.

Original duologues and one act plays were occasionally performed at these evenings, and it is a matter of interest to all who participated in the entertainments, that the first play Bennett wrote for performance was produced at a musical evening. And it came about in this way: Frederick Alcock had written a duologue for Mr. & Mrs. Stanley Hazell which was one of the surprise items. It was so cleverly written and acted that it was a marked success, and drew from Bennett the following letter:

9 Fulham Park Gardens,
13th February 1899
My dear Hazell,

I had a notion for a duologue last night. I have written it this evening, and now enclose it. I hope you may be able to read it; this is the rough draft. I have never before done a duologue for acting, though I have done several for print, and therefore I offer you this with some diffidence. If you don't like it you will say so. If you do, should you care to do it for my party on March 2nd?

Should this be so, I should like to witness a rehearsal. Perhaps you and Mrs. Hazell and Miss Draper could come here on the afternoon of the next musical evening, and we could go through it, But I do hope if you think it feeble you will say so.   ,

Don't disclose the plot to Fred or anyone.

With kind regards to all.
Yours fatiguedly
E.A. Bennett.

The sketch proved to be a very amusing little gem, entitled 'A Music Lesson', the characters 'He' and 'She', and a Maidservant, and occupied about a quarter of an hour.

18. IN HARMONY

A copy of the programme for *The Hundredth Musical Evening*, dated 20 April, 1901, which took place at 6 Victoria Grove, is held in the Potteries Museum and Art Gallery.[69] Looking back, the evening may be seen as the apotheosis of Marriott's musical evenings, which had begun with a small group of less than a dozen friends meeting occasionally, before blossoming into regular events attended by up to 40 people. It was Bennett's arrival on the scene that transformed the evenings into carefully planned events complete with printed programmes, an entertaining mix of serious and light-hearted performances, refreshments, and a stipulation of evening dress. Bennett's biographer Reginald Pound tells how this level of control and attention to detail extended to the domestic hearth: 'When Frederick Marriott went up to Burslem for Christmas with the Bennett family he found that Arnold Bennett imposed a similar routine on the festivities there. "You could hardly pull a cracker without first receiving a signal from Arnold."'[70]

Pound paints a warmly atmospheric picture of the 100th evening, an almost unique never to be forgotten moment when all of Bennett's closest friends, together with family members, were united in pleasure under one roof:

> We can picture the tinted coffee cups rising and falling on the tides of talk in the interval and imagine amusing scruples about the pose of the little finger in manipulating them.... Stanley Hazell, a popular member of the circle, sang his skittish song *In a Putney Garden*, parodying a Chelsea evening. There was more laughter when the studio was darkened for an illustrated humorous lecture entitled *Lantern Medley on One Sharpe*. Marriott told one of his customary parson stories in a voice suitably distorted for the purpose.... Bennett sang his 'Cider Song', remembered from schooldays and for which he provided his own vamping accompaniment on the piano. No one there would have believed that a day was to come when he would have the opportunity or the nerve to sing it from the stage of a London theatre, as he did in 1929.... The programme, opened by Herbert Sharpe playing 'Caprice on Ballet Airs from *Alceste*', was rounded off by 'General Entertainment by the Entire Company'.

It was the best of evenings, the best of all Marriott evenings; everyone said so, the departing guests exchanging loud appreciative sentiments as the echoes of their footsteps trailed away into the night under which a spring of the new century was flashing its lamp-lit green.[71]

There are a number of dimensions to Bennett's relationship to the musical culture of his time. As a child and young man he was exposed to a rich musical heritage in the Potteries.[72] This ranged from the singing he would have heard in the Methodist chapels, through public civic occasions, religious festivals, and chapel events accompanied by brass bands, to the more informal performances of popular songs and clog dancing witnessed in music-halls and public houses. Then there is Bennett as performer. His mother had given him some perfunctory piano lessons, but it wasn't until he felt the need to justify himself to the talented Marriott circle that he resumed serious study. Among his helpful mentors would certainly have been Herbert Sharpe, a founding member of the Royal College of Music and appointed Professor of Piano there in 1884, one year after it opened, and with Vaughan Williams as one of his pupils. Bennett dedicated *Anna of the Five Towns* (1902) to him: 'I dedicate this book with affection and admiration to Herbert Sharpe, an artist whose individuality and achievement have continually inspired me'.

The Sharpe family played an important role in expanding Bennett's musical knowledge and appreciation to cover an increasingly eclectic range of musical genres from Wagnerian opera to music-hall ditties. Mrs. Herbert Sharpe also played her part in encouraging Bennett to speak well-pronounced French, such that whilst never fluent he nevertheless felt confident enough to converse in the language when called upon. The Sharpe's son Cedric was to become a close friend from the moment he won a prize at age seven in *Woman* magazine, edited by Bennett. Cedric wrote to personally thank Bennett, saying that 'I had my photo taken with my cello. I will send you one as soon as the man sends them to mother'. Cedric maintained a close friendship with Bennett across the generations, going on to become a distinguished composer and cellist. In August 1909 Bennett gifted Cedric with the American first edition of his novel *The Statue* (1908), now in my possession, with a beautifully written pen inscription: 'To Cedric Sharpe, from his shamed partner in the crime of assassinating the string quartet of Schubert' in which the final 't' of Schubert morphs into an AB coat of arms. Marriott remarks that Bennett was especially fond of children and that in [the 1890s] he was 'Uncle Arnold' to numerous children in the neighbourhood to whom he was unrelated.[73]

19. THE GREAT ADVENTURE

At this time Wagner's operas had succeeded in getting a firm hold on the music-loving public, and members of our fraternity frequently attended the performances given at Covent Garden Opera House. Bennett used to get Herbert Sharpe, our chief musical star, to play through each opera a day or two before, in order that we should be the better able to follow, and understand the music.

Sharpe was an astonishingly expert sight-reader, and not only played the piano score, but he sang such of the vocal parts as came within the range of his voice. He could sing the bass and baritone parts in his natural voice, and he sang as much as he could of the soprano and tenor parts in falsetto, and we never ceased to marvel at his achievements. Getting Sharpe to prepare us in this way for the operas illustrates Bennett's inborn foresight and thoroughness.

I particularly remember one occasion, when we were preparing to go to Sharpe's house at Putney to hear him elucidate *Lohengrin*, Bennett said to me 'Frederick, let us walk there. I want to tell you the plot of a novel I am going to write'.

Of course I readily agreed, and we allowed ourselves a sufficient margin of time to get there without haste, and as we walked along he outlined the plan of the novel which he published some months later, under the title *Buried Alive*.

The story very ingeniously dealt with the complicated life of an artist and was of absorbing interest. I was amazed how completely he had got the scheme of it in his mind, although he hadn't commenced to write any part of it, or even put the plan of it on paper.

When I came to read the book after it was published, I was surprised to find how close it was in plan and detail to the scheme as he had originally told it to me. It was the book from which he afterwards constructed one of the most successful of his plays, *The Great Adventure*.

20. NOVEL IN MIND

Bennett's *Journal* entry for 13 February 1897 recalls that in 'either 1893 or 1894 I heard a Wagner opera for the first time. It was at Drury Lane and we sat in the balcony'.[74] He remembers that despite the excellence of the performance it was poorly attended with no more than 40 people in the balcony and the 'other parts of the building were similarly forlorn'. Three years on, and Bennett perfectly captures the dramatic change in British audiences' attitude to Wagner's music:

> To-night with [brother] Frank I went to a Wagner orchestral concert (promenade) at Queen's Hall, under Henry J. Wood. We got there a quarter of an hour before the commencement and already the entrance hall was packed with an eager tumultuous mass ... struggling to get to the ticket offices. At eight o'clock the vast floor (promenade) and the upper circle were crowded in every part, and in the balcony only a few reserved seats were left... The audience was enthusiastic, anticipatory... At the opening bars of 'The Flying Dutchman' overture I felt those strange tickling sensations in the back which are the physical signs of aesthetic emotion. [75]

Bennett's enthusiasm for attending operas (especially Wagner) and concerts never wavered throughout his life, and this love of music, and the response of audiences, found its way into many of his novels and stories, functioning as the prose equivalent of diegetic music on a film soundtrack. This aspect of his technique is first apparent in the serial *Love and Life*, published in 12 issues of the magazine *Hearth and Home* between 17 May and 2 August 1900. It was later revised and published in book form as *The Ghost* in 1907. Bennett's *Journal* entry for 24 January 1899 as he completes the text sounds a triumphant musical note: 'The writing of it has enormously increased my writing facility, and I now believe that I could do a similar novel in a month. It is, of the kind, good stuff, well written and well contrived, and some of the later chapters are really imagined, and, in a way, lyrical'.[76] This lyrical feeling, together with a clear indication of Bennett's early love for Wagner, finds full expression in *The Ghost*, Chapter 11, 'At the Opera':

> At eight o'clock, when the conductor appeared at his desk to an accompaniment of applauding taps from the musicians, the house

was nearly full. The four tiers sent forth a sparkle of diamonds, of silk, and of white arms and shoulders which rivalled the glitter of the vast chandelier. The wide floor of serried stalls ... added their more sombre brilliance to the show, while far above, stretching away indefinitely to the very furthest roof, was the gallery ... a mass of black spotted with white faces.

... The conductor raised his baton. The orchestra ceased its tuning. The lights were lowered. Silence and stillness enwrapped the auditorium. And the quivering violins sighed out the first chords of the *Lohengrin* overture. For me, then, there existed nothing save the voluptuous music, to which I abandoned myself as to the fascination of a dream. [77]

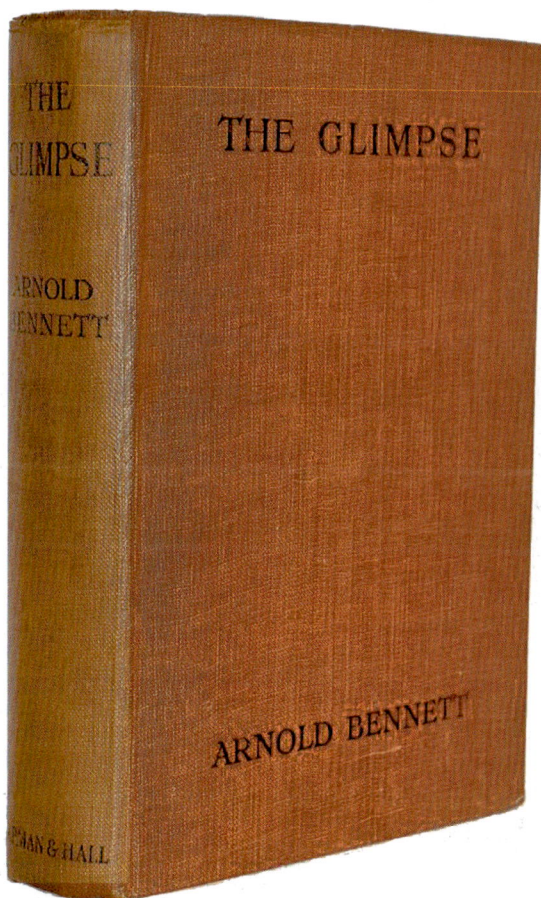

'Wagner, one used to hear, has dealt music such a blow that she must lie henceforward motionless forever.'

Arnold Bennett, *The Glimpse*.

21. BURGLARY

Three times we have been the victims of unwelcome attentions at the hands of burglars. By the law of averages it would seem that we have had more than our fair share of these visitations.

The second burglary happened while Arnold Bennett was living with us, and consequently he came in for a large part of the loss and annoyance. It took place while we were all away for a short holiday in Devonshire, and had left the house unattended.

Our friends Mr. & Mrs. Herbert Sharpe joined us in the expedition, and when they called for us on the morning of departure, Sharpe, at Bennett's suggestion, was persuaded to leave his overcoat behind in our house as the weather gave promise of warmth, and we weren't taking ours.

Fortunately our holiday wasn't curtailed by the burglar's nefarious enterprise, for it occurred in the early hours of the day on which we returned.

On arrival we were shocked to find every room in the house in the utmost state of disorder. All the locked drawers had been forced open and the contents emptied on to the floors. Locked cupboard doors and wardrobes were forced open and damaged in the process. Moreover, in the playful and approved manner of burglary technique, all the beds had been rumpled and rummaged in search of any valuables which might have been hidden in them.

A bottle containing certain liquid refreshment had disappeared from the sideboard cupboard in the dining room and was found beside the scullery sink, together with an empty glass.

We immediately reported the matter at the local Police Station, and they sent a detective and a constable to investigate it.

It was a curious feature of the affair, that a suit of Bennett's clothes, and Sharpe's overcoat were stolen, and exchanged for the old suit which the burglar left behind, while a suit of mine had evidently been tried on and discarded. This led the detective to the conclusion that he must be a big man; though the puzzling fact remained, that he had gone away in new stockings and shoes of mine, which were considered small even for a man of my short stature, (barely five feet three inches) and had left his old ones behind. He also left a 'Jemmy' constructed out of a large coarse file, turned up and sharpened at the end, with which he had forced an entrance, and opened drawers and cupboards. The 'Jemmy' and old clothes were taken away by the police, who thought they were good clues, but they never discovered the burglar.

My friends made great fun at my expense, because my clothes have twice been rejected by burglars on account of their being so small, but I claimed it as one of the advantages of being undersize.

Fortunately, our insurance policy covered burglary, so we were able to get compensation for the stolen goods; with the exception of Sharpe's overcoat, which of course we couldn't claim for.

While on the subject of thefts, I recall an amusing case which occurred about this time. Bennett used regularly to keep a box of dried figs in his room for his own casual consumption, but it appeared that the house-maid was also partial to figs, and couldn't resist the temptation of helping herself to the enticing fruit. As time went on the figs disappeared with increasing rapidity, so he adopted an ingenious plan for stopping the leakage. He placed in the box a card on which he had printed 'THOU GOD SEEST ME'. It was a very simple plan, but it was immediately successful in stopping the pilfering.

22. IN THE PICTURE

Break-ins and burglaries occur in several of Bennett's stories and novels. One such story, bearing a passing resemblance to Marriott's experience of finding his suit rejected as unsuitable by the thieves is 'The Christmas Eve Burglary', published in *Strand* magazine in December 1906, and reprinted in *The Grim Smile of the Five Towns* (1907). A local dignitary of the Five Towns, Sir Jehoshaphat Dain, has been presented with a portrait which neither he, his wife, nor, indeed, the presentation committee can initially stand the sight of. Opinions are only a little mollified by its critical reception at the Academy Exhibition where it is 'instantly hailed as possibly the most glorious masterpiece of modern times'.[78] The Dains remain unconvinced, and Sir Jehoshaphat takes the opportunity as chairman of the Borough bench of magistrates to declare a blatantly guilty burglar, William Smith, innocent. In the privacy of his chambers Sir Jehoshaphat then calls in a favour by arranging for Smith to break in and steal the detested portrait. Comes the agreed date, and Sir Jehoshaphat gets up early:

... and half-dressed, descended to the dining room just to see what sort of a mess William Smith had made.

The canvas of the portrait lay flat on the hearthrug, with the following words on it in chalk: 'This is no use to me'. It was the massive gold frame that had gone.

Further, as was later discovered, all the silver had gone. Not a spoon was left in the castle.[79]

Whilst the parallels with Marriott's case are not exact, they are close enough to allow today's reader a grim smile when s/he recalls the rather more successful destruction by its subject of Graham Sutherland's ill-fated portrait of Sir Winston Churchill, commissioned by the Houses of Parliament to mark Churchill's eightieth birthday.

Marriott concludes his chapter on 'Burglary' with a seemingly throw-away anecdote about Bennett's solution to preventing the suspected domestic pilfering of dried figs by a maid. But Bennett never discarded an amusing idea, and this particular party trick was to be put to good use in his film scenario and novel *Punch and Judy*, the hand-written manuscript of which I retrieved from the archive at Pennsylvania State University. It was transcribed and published in 2012.

The anti-hero of the story, Mr. Henry Flitfoot, noticing that cigars have a habit of vanishing from their box, confides in his secretary, Miss Sligo, little realizing that she is the culprit:

> Mr. Flitfoot was not very long after Miss Sligo that morning; but he did not arrive before she had collated all the Curtiss documents for him from the various departments of the office. He glanced through them quickly.
>
> 'Everything appears to be in order,' said he.
>
> 'Not appears in order,' she replied. 'Is in order.'
>
> Mr. Flitfoot opened his cigar cabinet.
>
> 'Someone appears to be pinching my cigars,' said he.
>
> 'Not appears to be pinching them. Is pinching them,' said she smiling.
>
> 'You've noticed it?'
>
> 'I have.'
>
> 'Who can it be?'
>
> 'Even if I knew I shouldn't say. I never tell against the staff.'
>
> "What am I to do?"

'I was going to put this piece of paper inside the cabinet.'

Miss Sligo produced a typewritten sheet, which contained the following words:

'I have counted these cigars.'

Mr. Flitfoot laughed as he lit a cigar.

'If you will initial it,' she suggested.

Mr. Flitfoot initialled the paper and put it inside the cabinet.

'You are a genius, Sligo,' said he.

'If you say it,' said she.[80]

Marriott has nothing to say on the subject of Bennett's involvement with the film industry, and yet it would be remiss not to give it due weight here, as equal to his fascination with the world of music. The memoir mentions that Bennett's novel *Buried Alive* was adapted for the stage by its author as *The Great Adventure,* but does not go on to say that two silent film versions of the play were released in 1916 and 1921. In addition to *The Great Adventure* there were silent film adaptations of *The Grand Babylon Hotel* (1914), *Sacred and Profane Love* (1921), *The Old Wives' Tale* (1921), *The Card* (1922) and *The City of Pleasure* (1929), all of which had worldwide distribution. Bennett loved going to the cinema as much as the opera, although his *Journal* entries on both could be scathing if he thought a production fell short of his own high standards. It is only recently, that the full extent of Bennett's aesthetic and financial interest in early twentieth-century film has become apparent.

There is in fact a strong case to be made for regarding Bennett as the first and most important professionally engaged writer to bring the world of cinema and film into serious fiction. The publication of *The Regent* in 1913 marks one of the earliest references to film in the English novel, with a short but accurate passage on the cinematograph's invasion of the music-hall in the Five Towns. More importantly, *The Price of Love* (1914), set in Bursley/Burslem, has a unique claim to be the first English literary novel to explore the central importance of cinema to provincial popular culture. It celebrates the Oriental-inspired architecture of the first purpose-built cinema palaces, describes their programming, considers the makeup of the audience, and lays bare the machinations of the commercial funding of cinema expansion .The very real original structure of Bennett's fictional Imperial cinema still stands on Burslem's Moorland Road, only now the plush interior has been ripped out to accommodate 'Pickerings of Burslem, Fishing Tackle Specialists'.

Bennett began writing his own first film scenario, *The Wedding Dress*, in 1920, but despite its obvious potential cinematic merits it fell victim to the general malaise of the post-war British film industry and the increasing in-roads being made by American film imports.[81] It wasn't until the release of *Piccadilly* (1929), directed by E.A. Dupont, that Bennett's talents as a screenwriter were given full expression. Today the film is recognized as one of the last great British silent movies. The British Film Institute's digitally restored print received a world premiere in front of a sell-out audience at the October 2003 New York Film Festival, with the Festival's programme note describing it as a 'thrilling cinematographic jewel and a landmark in the emancipation of a non-white actress [Anna May Wong]'.[82] This then, in Margaret Drabble's estimation, was 'the Arnold Bennett who was ever ready to take on the new, the modernist Bennett who enjoyed the challenge of the future.'[83]

Anna May Wong (1905-1961)

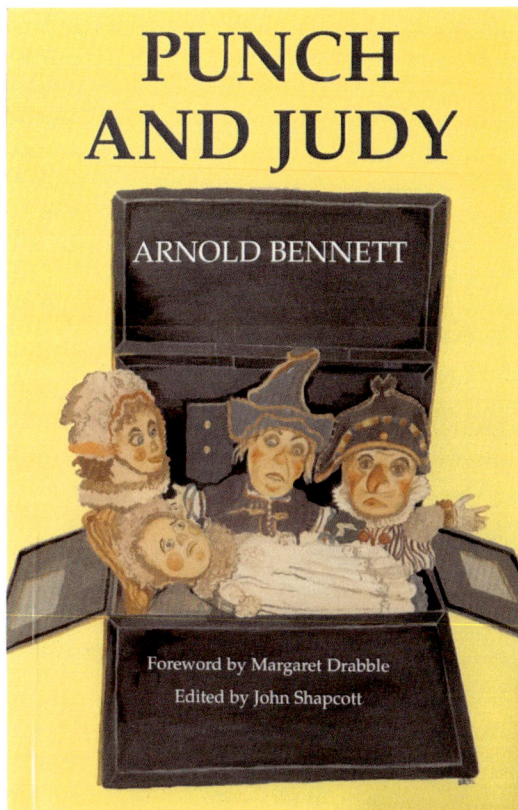

PUNCH AND JUDY

ARNOLD BENNETT

Foreword by Margaret Drabble
Edited by John Shapcott

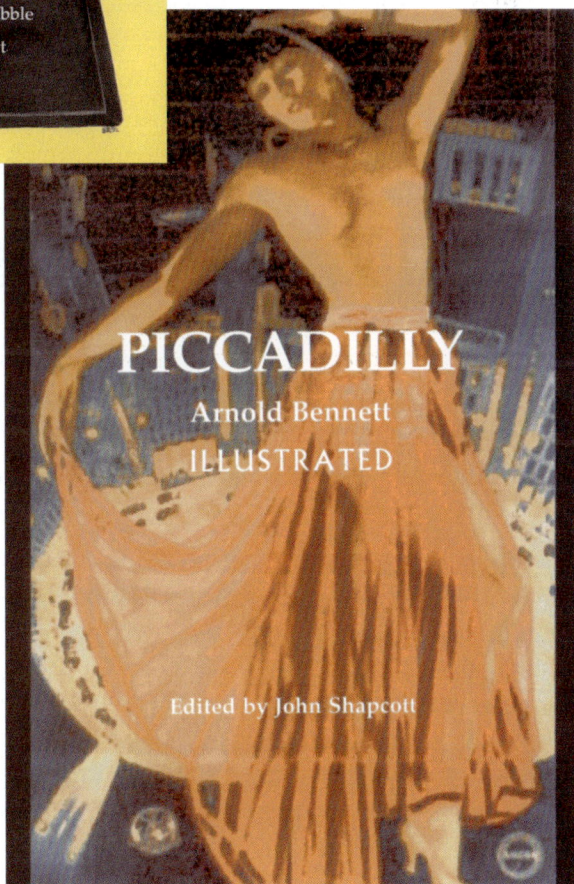

PICCADILLY

Arnold Bennett

ILLUSTRATED

Edited by John Shapcott

23. THE DERBY

I had my first experience of a 'Race Meeting' about forty years ago when I went with Arnold Bennett to the Derby.

All the newspapers, morning, evening, weekly, and even the Sunday papers had for some time been giving the subject of the forthcoming Derby great prominence, and we agreed that it was a spectacle that we ought to see, at least once; so we decided to take the day off and spend it at Epsom. A novel experiment for both of us.

Our ignorance of horse-racing matters was complete, and we were attracted to the Derby more from the spectacular point of view than anything else. We weren't particularly interested in either owners or jockeys, and we had no money at stake in the way of bets or sweepstake tickets, so we were quite indifferent as to which of the horses won or lost.

There are few places better adapted for the display of vast crowds of people and the pageantry associated with horse-racing than the Epsom Downs, and we were not disappointed by what the most popular racing event of the year had to offer in this direction. Indeed, we were amazed.

Never before had we seen such a vast concourse of humanity gathered together in such a suitable and picturesque setting; a crowd which included all types indiscriminately drawn from all grades of society, and from all parts of the world.

We arrived on the course some time before the racing commenced, and we moved about amongst the noisy, hustling 'Bookies' with their raucous ear-splitting voices, each one trying to shout louder than his neighbour, and inviting us to patronise 'the old firm'; and we were assailed by tricksters of many kinds who tried, without success, to extort money from us on the promise of huge profits.

The gipsy proprietors of showily painted caravans, many of whom professed to tell fortunes, pestered us for sixpences in exchange for their estimates of our characters, and forecasts of what the future held in store for us, but we resisted all their efforts.

The fantastic costumes worn by many of the regular race-goers added to the brilliance of the kaleidoscopic panorama. Costers with their wives and families, all wearing clothes richly decorated from head

The 1896 Derby.

to foot with patterns worked in pearl buttons of varying sizes, so closely laid that only small portions of the foundation cloth or velvet remained visible. Their women-folk wore large hats generously trimmed with ostrich feathers of liberal length. Purple velvet seemed to be the favourite material for their frocks and their necks were encircled with bright coloured wraps.

Their mode of transit was by donkey chaise, and on such special occasions as Derby Day, the donkeys were carefully groomed, and their trappings were ornamented with bright coloured rosettes and ribbons. When these vehicles were fully loaded, they presented a very lively appearance, and made an animated note in the thronged procession of conveyances to and from the course in every direction.

The 'Pearlie' still maintains a place in the social scheme of the East End of London, and their elaborate dress can be seen on parade there, but not in such profusion as they could in those days.

Every section of the race-course claimed our attention, from the starting point to the winning-post, and we viewed the downs and the races from many stand-points.

First we took up a position as near the winning post as we could get, only to find that the crowd was so dense that we could scarcely see anything of the horses as they passed, but we were impressed by the astonishing way in which the experienced race-goer could pick out both horses and jockeys as they flashed by, shouting out their names and positions, while our untrained eyes registered nothing more than a very blurred image.

It brought to my mind how the early Japanese artists had so trained their vision, that they had been able to record the varied and curious positions of the wings of birds in flight, long before the photographic camera revealed them to Western people. After the passing of so many years, some of the most complete impressions emerging are those centred round the starting points of the races. There were fewer people round that part of the course, and the time occupied in getting the horses into line, afforded us a good opportunity of watching their beautiful and spirited movements, and the skilful way they were handled by their riders.

Throughout Arnold Bennett's career he was able to turn every new experience to some journalistic or literary use, and one result of this, his first visit to a race meeting, was the appearance of a record of his impressions under the pseudonym 'Gwendolin' in one of the series of social paragraphs he was regularly contributing to the woman's magazine he was editing at the time. He made frequent use of his note book as we roamed about during the intervals between the races.

Later on he became increasingly interested in the best exhibitions of skill in all kinds of sport, and made a point of witnessing the greatest contests, and often made subject matter for his pen out of the events.

24. CONFUSION

Bennett signed articles for Woman as 'E.A.B.', 'E.A. Bennett', 'Jim's Wife', 'Barbara', and 'Sarah Volatile', but never, as suggested by Marriott, as 'Gwendolin'. The profusion of pseudonyms adopted by Bennett in the early years of his career has long caused confusion among biographers and critics, largely because, as Anita Miller has argued in her seminal *Arnold Bennett: An Annotated Bibliography, 1887-1932*, (1977), none has ever gone back to the original archive sources to read and comment upon the some 1,026 articles published during the first ten years of his London career. Bennett himself indicated the difficulties involved in assigning text to author in his August 1927 *Harper's Bazar* article, 'Editing a Woman's Paper': 'My articles on new books were of so advanced a kind that they might have ruined the paper [*Woman*] had they been read. Similarly with criticisms of the drama ... Occasionally I wrote on picture exhibitions and on concerts in the same strain. (I had various pseudonyms).[84] To add further confusion we find Marguerite Bennett claiming erroneously that 'articles were signed by women's names only, including those which he himself wrote and signed Ida, Rose, Jane , Edith, Dorothy or whatever it might be'[85] One of Bennett's earliest serious critics, Georges Lafourcade, set in motion the mistaken belief that there was a Bennett/Gwendoline, or Gwendolen, or even Marriott's Gwendolin, that persisted for over 40 years: 'He wrote anonymously or under unexpected signatures (Gwendolene!) on practically everything, frocks, lingerie, bargains, food, cookery, children, hygiene and Paris "high life."'[86]

But for sure the greatest culprit in misleading biographers and critics who neglected to read just a few issues of *Woman* held in readily available bound copies at the British Newspaper Library was Bennett himself, who knowingly and mischievously led innocent readers into a labyrinthine identity cul-de-sac in *The Truth about an Author*:

> The editor was enchanted with my social paragraphs; he said I was born to it, and perhaps I was. I innocently asked in what part of the paper they were to shine.
>
> 'Gwendolen's column,' he replied.
>
> 'Who is Gwendolen?'I demanded. Weeks before, I had admired Gwendolen's breadth of view and worldly grasp of things, qualities rare in a woman.
>
> 'You are,' he said, 'and I am. It's only an office signature.'[87]

All of which, especially the assertion that Bennett's 1890s articles contained material unfairly neglected by generations of literary critics, provides me with an opportunity here to select just one of his many illuminating literary/sociological articles. This example, signed Barbara, appeared in the 11 August 1897 issue of *Woman* as part of Bennett's wide-ranging regular 'Book Chat' column, and lays claim for inclusion in any compendium or Companion to Brontë studies:

Parallel Lives

****

THE BRONTË RELICS AT HAWORTH

Last week I cycled from London to a part of the world known as the West Riding of Yorkshire. It is a remarkable place. For the completeness of its hospitality, and the quaint wonder of its dialect, I imagine it to be unsurpassed in England; but its roads - its roads are unique for utter and prodigious badness. Within a radius of ten miles from Halifax I found only one stretch of level, and that stretch was paved with the most abominable stony inequalities possible to be conceived. The cyclist in the West Riding does not cycle; he just makes his machine jump from crag to crag. On these roads tyres don't puncture; they burst - probably out of simple weariness; I have caught them in the act of bursting, and mended them afterwards.

But this is not Miss Swift's 'Cycling Gossip'. What I set out to say was that I happened to be staying in Halifax, and that Keighley being near Halifax, and Howarth near Keighley, I naturally had a desire to visit the home of the Brontës, and the museum of Brontë relics of which one has heard so much. I cycled, with infinite labour, to Keighley, and then, hearing bad accounts of the roads further on, it seemed good to me to deposit my fatigued machine in the cloak-room and fare forward by train. The train journey to Haworth is not inspiring. And Haworth itself is not inspiriting. I had always pictured it as an infinitesimal hamlet, six miles from any place where pen nibs might be bought. Nothing of the kind. It narrowly escapes being a town. On leaving the station the first thing that one sees is a huge mill, from which issue mill-girls whose faces are prettier than their manners. The second thing one sees is a vast new school. The third thing one sees is a ribbon of grim, grey stone houses, carelessly flung down upon the side of a steep hill. That ribbon is Haworth, the Haworth of the Brontës.

At the top one finds the church, and the parsonage, whose front windows enjoy the close prospect of a crowded and yet desolate churchyard. When one has seen the parsonage and the churchyard, one realises why the Brontë sisters dealt only with the tragic, why their stories move in an atmosphere of intense and passionate gloom, why their humour is so cruelly sardonic, and why their own lives were set about on every side by adverse fates. In the nature of things it could not and should not have been otherwise. These strange, lonely girls, curious mixture of modernity and the antique prejudices of the time, were born

98

to infelicity in order that therewith they might be great artists, and those parsonage windows were an essential part of the scheme - , the remoteness, the painful sordid ascent, the harsh people, and the naked grey-green hills. Imagine Haworth Parsonage in Winter, when the snow drifts up against the gravestones; imagine it in summer, when the sad trees, with all their leaves, cannot hide away the tombs, and then you will understand *Wuthering Heights*, and the ponderous shadows of *Shirley*, and the dreadful passion of *Villette*.

Quite close to the church is the museum, a small room over the local bank, to see which one pays threepence. As I entered, the attendant was studiously immersed in a book, and the book was *Jane Eyre*. Whether he read *Jane Eyre* from a dreadful sense of fitness or for mere pleasure I had not the courage to enquire; but the sight of him so engaged made me laugh. The collection of relics has deep and real interest. It relates, of course, chiefly to Charlotte, and as regards her it must be pretty nearly complete. It contains not only her manuscripts and her (atrociously bad) pencil drawings and water-colour sketches, but also such things as the engraved collar worn by her dog, her work-basket, the cup out of which she drank tea, the urn in which the tea was made; and all these trifles help one to construct one's own private picture of the life at the parsonage. It contains a copy of the prospectus of the establishment for young ladies kept by the Misses Brontë at Haworth. Oh, most quaint prospectus! How I should have liked to carry you away, with your queer note: - 'Each young lady to be provided with one pair of sheets, pillow-cases, four towels, a dessert and teaspoon!' Surely your syntax is a little rocky! Can it be that the brain that created Rochester condescended to draw up a little piffling absurdity like you? The most pathetic exhibit is the obituary notice of Charlotte, which appeared in the great local paper, the *Leeds Mercury*. This notice, perfunctory even in its praise, consisted of exactly eight lines! Nowadays the *Leeds Mercury* would be proud to give eight times eight lines to the death of Charlotte's second cousin's great niece, if ever Charlotte had one, merely because she was Charlotte's second cousin's grand-niece.

I must not forget the public-house. There are three public-houses within five yards of the museum, but I mean the 'Black Bull,' where Branwell Brontë (whom the people of the district seem to regard with peculiar veneration) used to sit and smoke and drink, and talk to an appreciative audience. There, in the corner of the parlour, is an old oak chair, sacred now to his memory - a chair which pilgrims to the shrine make a point of occupying, so that they may say afterwards: 'I sat in it.' Having duly sat in the chair, one goes forth into the street, stares into the window of an emporium of 'Brontë Perfumes' and 'Presents from Haworth', and then slides gingerly away down the steep street to the accompaniment of personal remarks from the inhabitants. There is nothing more to be seen.

****

Bennett set out on his epic cycle ride to Yorkshire in the company of his two good friends, Fred Alcock and Herbert Sharpe, on 31 July 1897. With the 'Book Chat' view of Howarth to hand, what strikes the reader of Bennett's *Journal* entries is the contrast with his sunny view of the places seen prior to reaching Yorkshire:

> Riding through the heart of England, the general impression is one of decent prosperity and content. One sees nothing of that agricultural distress of which one reads so much in towns. It is an endless succession of picturesque and cleanly rural activities punctuated by neat towns, where old-fashioned inns seem to dominate and represent the municipal architecture. The worst roads are passable, and every village has the air of being well-tended. [88]

All of which contrasts sharply with Bennett's dismissive assessment of Howarth's amenities, and of his contempt for the commodification of literature and the early evidence of the rising tide of associated tourist tat.

But to return to Marriott's subject of horse racing with which this chapter began. By coincidence Bennett's *Journal* entry for 2 August on the Lincolnshire leg of their ride reports that:

> The landlord of the *Reindeer* told us at length of his difficulties with the swell-roughs in race-weeks, and it appeared that at these times a loaded revolver always formed part of his personal outfit. 'This place is simply hell,' he said. 'We have two policemen continually at the foot of the stairs, and at any moment eight more can be summoned in 15 seconds.' [89]

The landlord's opinion of race-goers is echoed 30 years later by Lord Furber, musing on suitable pastimes for a bored millionaire, in Bennett's novel *The Strange Vanguard:* "'There's racing. Scoundrels behind ye. Snobs in front of ye. If the jockey's to be trusted the horse isn't. Ye can have racing.'"[90]

It would appear, on the evidence of Bennett's story 'In the Capital of the Sahara', that they organize these things better abroad:

Once a year, in February, Biskra becomes really and excessively excited, and the occasion is its annual two-day race-meeting. Then the tribes and their chieftains and their camels arrive magically out of the four corners of the desert and fill the oasis. And the English, French, and Germans arrive from the Mediterranean coast, with their trunks and their civilisation, and crowd the hotels till beds in Biskra are precious beyond rubies. And under the tropical sun, East and West meet magnificently on the racecourse to the North of the European reserve. And the tribesmen, their scraggy steeds trailing superb horsecloths, are arranged in hundreds behind the motor-cars and landaus, with the *pari-mutuel* in full swing twenty yards away. And the dancing-girls, the renowned Ouled-Nails, covered with gold coins and with muslin in high, crude, violent purples, greens, vermilions, shriek and whinny on their benches just opposite the grand stand, where the Western women ... quiz them through their glasses.[91]

Bennett goes on to paint a vivid picture of the surrounding scenery in the 'heart of the mysterious and unchangeable Sahara',[92] before coming to the race itself. 'The competing horsemen appeared round the bend for the last time, the dancing-girls whinnied in their high treble, the crowd roared, and the Prix de la Ville was won and lost'.[93]

This story and the race meeting it describes is particularly important in illuminating a little known period in Bennett's life when, at the beginning of 1903, he left England for a month's holiday in Algeria. He was accompanied for part of the time by his friend Eden Phillpotts, but otherwise he was alone and kept no journal; apart from three postcards home all other contemporary documents are either none existent or have been lost. This was a difficult time for Bennett following the death of his father in January 1902, and the return of his mother to Burslem from his leased Bedfordshire farm. Bennett's decision to leave England, and his subsequent journey, have been forensically detailed by Nicholas Redman who travelled in Bennett's footsteps, using clues from stories, novels and articles. His article 'Bennett in Algeria'[94] is the most authorative account we have of this otherwise tantalizing lacuna in Bennett's biography.

25. PICK-POCKETS

It was not an uncommon experience in the early days of our association, to find ourselves waiting in a queue for the pit doors of some theatre to open, for neither of us could afford the more expensive bookable seats. On one occasion when Bennett and I were waiting at the pit entrance of the Savoy Theatre, to attend the performance of one of the Gilbert and Sullivan Operas, we were busy reading our evening papers, when two men made a disturbance by crushing up uncomfortably close. These waves of pressure were repeated several times, and after one of our remonstrances, one of the men said 'I am darned sick of waiting here', and then he and his friend walked away; much to our relief.

When at last the doors were opened, and we were comfortably settled in our seats, Bennett, on putting his hand into one of his coat pockets, made the startling discovery that there was an empty purse in it. As the purse didn't belong to either of us, it was evident that the two men who had engineered the crushing in the queue were pick-pockets, and had stolen somebody's purse, abstracted the contents, and then placed the empty purse into Bennett's pocket. When we had recovered from our astonishment, we each explored our pockets in fear lest we had been robbed, and we were relieved to find that we hadn't lost anything.

Speaking of the incident afterwards to the police constable to whom we handed the purse, he told us that it was a common practice of pick-pockets to dispose of purses they had stolen in this way, so that there would not be any incriminating evidence found upon them if they happened to be caught.

****

RESTORED TEXT

Some months afterwards, while we were sitting with several friends round the fire in one of Bennett's rooms; which served him in the triple capacity of library, study and sitting-room; the adventure with pick-pockets was mentioned, and nearly all those present could relate stories of their friends who had been robbed by thieves.

A discussion followed on the great skill of expert thieves, and particularly of the pick-pocket branch of the profession. I ventured the opinion that it was one of the easiest of crafts, and said that I had many times indulged in it for the fun of the thing, and the pleasure of watching the surprised look on the face of the victim when the property was restored. However, none of them supported my view, so later on, at one of our musical evenings, I again put my theory to the test. I went up to one of my friends who had a valuable pearl pin in his tie, and drawing his attention to some imaginary dust on his left shoulder, I extracted the pin while his head was turned.

I then walked away and got another friend to similarly look over his shoulder while I deftly put the pin in his tie. There was no difficulty in making the exchange, and I have many times performed similar purloining exploits by way of fun, with varying success. I am convinced that if pocket picking were really a difficult job, many more thousands of operators would be caught in the act.

I have never attempted to pick Arnold Bennett's pockets, but I confess to having often picked his brains.

****

26. A FROLIC OF HIS OWN

Writing to J. B. Pinker from France in April 1904, Bennett concludes a long letter with the news that: 'I am happy to say that I have begun a sensational serial compared to which the *Grand Babylonian Hotel* is nothing. Its title is simply & majestically *'HUGO'*. It will be immense'.[95] Published in *To-Day magazine* in 12 instalments between 3 May-9 July 1905, before book publication in 1906, *Hugo: A Fantasia on Modern Themes* certainly took on one of the 'immense' developments of modernity, namely the department store. The Paris arcades began to appear post-1822 with the boom in the textile trade, and soon became a centre of commerce in luxury items. Bennett would have known and delighted in the Parisian arcades department stores, appreciating Walter Benjamin's opinion that 'in fitting them out, art enters into the servant of the merchant'.[96] With conspicuous display attracting crowds of wealthy customers came also the temptation and opportunity for crime. In Bennett's novel there is a plot to disrupt the smooth operation of Hugo's new store by the deployment of thieves and pickpockets every bit as skilled as the amateur Marriott:

> [The heroine, Lily] had not proceeded twenty yards before she was stopped by a group of persons round a policeman - a policeman obviously called in from Sloane Street. A stout lady of lady-like appearance had been arrested on a charge of attempted pocket-picking. An accusatory shopwalker charged her, and she replied warmly that she was Lady Brice (*née Kentucky-Webster*), the American wife of the well-known philanthropist, and that her carriage was waiting outside. The policeman and the shopwalker smiled. It was so easy to be the wife of a well-known philanthropist, and in these days all the best pickpockets had their carriages waiting outside.[97]

Lady Brice's false arrest is the result of a plan by the novel's villain, Ravengar, 'to sow the place with pickpockets' so as to 'arrange for the arrest of important customers on preposterous charges of theft'.[98] Pickpockets apart, the above short excerpt is doubly interesting in the way Bennett plants Lady Brice to neatly imply the international appeal of the London fashion market, at the same time as signalling his own Socialist beliefs in an ironic comment on the wealth of philanthropists with carriages who might well have accumulated capital by the legitimate pocket picking of labour.

Incidentally, this novel of 'modern themes' further lives up to its sub-title with a sabotage plot that hinges on the playing of a phonograph record. In a key chapter entitled 'What the Phonograph Said', Bennett allows the uncanniness of voice technology to supposedly imitate the voice of a dead man. Bennett's interest in modern technology is apparent in several of his novels and non-fiction texts - his descriptions of the American telephone system in his 1912 travel book *Your United States* being a prime example. An unknown telephone caller sees Hugo pondering the invisible reach of modern technology: 'Hugo wondered where the man could be. And the sinister magic of the telephone, which brought this sad quiet voice to him from somewhere out of the immensity of England, but which would not yield up to him the secret of its hiding, struck him strangely'.[99] And this 'strangeness' would infiltrate the spy fiction of the twentieth century.

27. HOCKLIFFE

At various times Bennett seemed to tire of town life and sought the countryside for the opportunities it afforded of quietude for his work, and for taking exercise in the open air.

When making his selection of a house, he was always careful that it should provide sufficient accommodation to admit of his having friends to stay with him whenever he desired company.

He made his first venture of this kind by renting a farm house at Hockliffe near Dunstable, and I spent many jolly weekends there. Indeed, it is no exaggeration to say that all his more intimate friends enjoyed the amenities of the Hockliffe farm house while Bennett lived there. His friend Rickards was a fairly frequent visitor and indulged freely in horse-riding exercise. I have vivid recollections of being persuaded by Bennett to mount a horse, and as it was my first equestrian experience, I had an exciting time, and after careering about for a quarter of an hour or so, while the horse succeeded in meeting me half way at every bounce, I found that I was much more comfortable standing up than sitting down

Marriott attributes this caricature to Rickards but other commentators ascribe it to Sir William Nicholson.

By permission of Dr. H. V. Lancaster

BENNETT IN THE COUNTRY, CARICATURED BY A FRIEND

for a day or two afterwards. It had the effect of permanently curing me of any desire for further indulgence in that particular form of exercise.

At Hockliffe, Bennett affected a garb which was something of a cross between such as was worn by gentlemen farmers and country Squires, and for a house dog he invested in a huge St. Bernard, which had such an excess of saliva, that it constantly overflowed from the corners of its capacious mouth, leaving drip-marks in its course!

The accompanying caricature by Rickards gives a fair impression of Bennett and his dog at that time.

28. COUNTRY LIFE

The Bedfordshire farmhouse Marriott refers to is Trinity Hall Farm, a rather gaunt building on the edge of Hockcliffe village. Built of yellowish brick, with a slate roof, its unprepossessing appearance was compensated for by its magnificent location commanding clear views over many miles of the Bedfordshire Chilterns. A private drive lined it to the historic main road of Watling Street:

> 'The scenery, however, is very Great, & Great are the villages. Greatest of all is Watling Street, sweeping past my meadow ... in a stupendous straight line. What I like about Watling Street is its sublime disregard of everything except direction. It "goes for" Holyhead with its head down, & it gets there, either over hills or through 'em doesn't matter which'.[100]

This musing of Bennett's reads to me very much like the unconscious mindset of a man checking his escape route from countryside to town should the need arise, and, indeed, the same letter goes on to paint a revealing picture of his active disinterest in the practicalities of rural living:

> I shall never be *interested* in gardens. I want a nice garden (& shall have one) & a horse that will go (& have got one), but I don't want to be troubled with the details ... I have no *real* interest in anything except eating, writing, music, & the graphic arts. And never shall have ... I would sooner play a piano duet than understand about inflorescences, & I would sooner write about digging than dig. When the gardener ... begins to hold forth to me about the garden, I feel the *dis*-interest creep over me, & it makes me shudder... Let the

garden be there, but I only want to walk on it, with my feet &
eyes.[101]

Some 18 months later and the notion of playing the part of country
squire seems to be wearing very thin, even that 'goer' of a horse adding
to Bennett's disenchantment. In a remarkable piece of insightful self-
analysis, Bennett writes to the same correspondent:

I think I am never happy, & I don't expect to be. I am continually
kidding myself that I shall be happy when I have done a certain
thing. I do it, & then begin over again to kid that I shall be happy
when I have done something else. So it runs. I have written one
good novel this year.... My sole consolation in this world of unrest is
that I do naively admire a lot of my own work...
   I ruptured myself partly with riding & partly with [? Pumping]
immediately afterwards. I am quite comfortable now in a truss.[102]

The 'one good novel' completed at Hockcliffe was *Anna of the Five
Towns* (1902). More immediately relevant to his time at Trinity Farm is
Teresa of Watling Street, published as a serial in the *Golden Penny*
magazine between 4 July and 19 September 1903, and in book form in
1904. Dismissed at the time by the *Manchester Guardian*'s reviewer as
'readable trash', it has fared little better at the hands of subsequent critics
who have either ignored it or considered it aesthetically irredeemable.
Bennett himself claimed to be embarrassed by it, later in his career
attempting to suppress its publication. As late as October 1928, in a letter
to E.V. Lucas (on the staff of publishers Methuen), he was still disowning
the book as 'the world's worst novel'.[103]

   Yet a detailed close reading might conclude that it is not without its
merits. Among these are the attractive glimpses of a recognizable
Bedfordshire countryside that seduced Bennett into believing that he
could be content and productive without the constant attractions of the
metropolis:

The day was jocund, the landscape smiled; in the forty acre field
below the house a steam-plough, actuated by two enormous
engines and a steel hawser, was working at the bidding of a farmer
who farmed on principles of his own, and liked to do his ploughing
at midsummer. The steam-plough rattled and jarred and jolted like
a humorous and high-spirited leviathan; the birds sang merrily
above it; the Chiltern Hills stretched away in the distance, bathed in

limitless glad sunshine; and Watling street ran white, dazzling, and serene, down the near slope and up the hill towards Dunstable, curtained in the dust of rural traffic.[104]

But Bennett's knowledge of the pitfalls of commerce and the insidious powers of banks, gleaned from life in The Potteries, and powerfully delineated in *Anna of the Five Towns*, spills over into the supposed rural idyll of *Teresa of Watling Street* with a satiric take on capitalism's ready acceptance of the manipulation of financial markets and stock valuations by unscrupulous dealers. These are themes that will continue to colour his fantasias on modern life, his non-fiction, and his literary fiction, finding full expression in his last completed novel, *Imperial Palace* (1930). This latter includes a textually innovative shareholders' meeting that harks back to the opening sentence of *Teresa of Watling Street*: 'Since money is the fount of all modern romantic adventure, the City of London, which holds more money to the square yard than any other place in the world, is the most romantic of cities.'

Finance, politics, and passion are also very much to the fore in the scenario for a play, *The Crime*, which was intended to be a collaboration with H.G. Wells, but which in the event never materialized. When Bennett wrote a short letter of admiration to Wells in September 1897 it sparked the beginning of a life-long friendship between two men from similar backgrounds but with very different personalities. From the moment Bennett first visited Wells at his Sandgate home in Kent they never lost touch with each other, even though their views often diverged. Given this coming together of two such eminent writers it is indeed a crime that the proposed collaboration simply fizzled out for no apparent reason other, perhaps, than Bennett's failure to negotiate satisfactory terms with Frederick Harrison, the manager of the Haymarket Theatre. At the outset Wells was somewhat indifferent about the project, but perfectly willing to leave his friend to undertake the initial work, writing on 22 February, 1902:

I don't altogether jump at *The Crime*. It's dissipation. Still if you do quite clearly mean to do all the work and let me come in 'without hindrance to present occupation' it's tempting - wife and child - boots very old now - trousers so thin in seat as to give rise to chills - aged mother in the workhouse - mortgage on my bicycle - garden roller in pawn. Yes. You get a commission for it and I'll give you seven clear days of honest collaboration.[105]

Within two days Bennett has replied from Hockcliffe that if Wells could spare but half a day to develop the scenario he 'could write the piece by myself in 7 days'. Then a further seven months elapse as the idea lies dormant until Bennett writes again from Hockcliffe that he is 'prepared to offer to pay you half of all I make out of *The Crime* up to £1,000, if you care to turn it over to me absolutely. I have absolutely no scruples about taking another man's ideas under the wing of my own name in a case of this kind'.[106]

But by this time the formerly luke-warm Wells has become a more enthusiastic would-be collaborator:

I feel strongly that *The Crime* is rather too good a thing to drop. I think you make a fair offer about taking it over, but on the whole I'd rather I think see it through. But I don't see any chance of getting really to work at it until 1903. It's all nonsense to say it would only take me a week. I don't work that way. Suppose you go through it, amplify the scenario, get in some key lines and in fact write a sort of latticework of the play. Get this done in duplicate, send me a copy and use the other to negotiate. I'll turn the whole thing over in my mind and (if I may) come down to Hockcliffe either in Dec 1902 or Jan 1903. I think we want a different relationship of the murderer and the woman. I feel if we let things go down to the subconscious for a bit it will come up stronger and richer.[107]

Bennett proceeded as Wells suggested, but the collaborative meeting at Hockcliffe never took place. The only known surviving copy of *The Crime* is Bennett's handwritten pen manuscript in The Potteries Museum & Art Gallery, where I experienced the very real archive-hunter's thrill of unearthing it whilst helping in cataloguing the Museum's Bennett Collection.

The Crime
a play in 4 acts

scenario
by
Arnold Bennett

Characters
****

John Lethaby. millionaire financier who is murdered at the beginning of the play.

Arthur Norris. a man of means, artistic, nervous; aged 35.

William Stanway. a rising financier, calm, determined powerful, aged 40

Lewis Folkard M.P. (of "Folkards" house furnishers, Tottenham Court Road.) a pompous political ass, fat, puffy, aged 55.

Frank Micheldever. A young stockbroker. nervous, excitable, exuberant, clever. aged 28.

Paterson. Lethaby's doddering old clerk.

Lilian Norris. wife of Arthur Norris; of interesting appearance, charming, with plenty of character beneath, aged 30.

Annie Folkard. daughter of Folkard M.P. a girl of gracious carriage: sympathetic but restrained in manner; calm; equal to crisis; with tremendous reserve of will, aged 25.

Mrs. Folkard. wife of Folkard M.P.

Act I
Office of Letherby, the millionaire financier in the city. 6pm

Act II
Private dining room in the Grand Babylon Hotel. 7.30pm

Act III
Room in Norris's flat. 11pm.

Note

Imagine this as the sensational story of a murder, put on the stage. Its interest is not only melodramatic but psychological throughout. It will have an air of being absolutely true to life while retaining a quality of thrilling. All details are to be realistic. The whole of the three acts pass on one single evening. This I think is a new thing on the modern stage. Stagely effective 'curtains' are purposely avoided in order to aid the effect of truthfulness.

My aim is to raise the tense interest of the audience and to keep them tightly strung up till the final scene.

The scenario is very short & only pretends to give the main outlines of the piece.

Act I
Lethaby's office

A green curtain rises, disclosing a blank act drop. Voices indistinctly heard behind the act drop, a sharp movement, the crack of a revolver, a cry, hurried footsteps & the slamming of a door.

Act drop rises.

The scene is the luxuriously furnished office of Lethaby in the city, brilliantly lighted by electricity. Time, about 6 pm, afternoon in late autumn. Door at centre of back. This door is not properly shut & someone behind tries to shut it quietly & then bangs it. Principal effects in room a large writing table, desk, a large easy chair with ear-flaps near desk, & a large draught screen. In the chair is the dead body of Lethaby. The right hand of the corpse rests on the table; the left is on the arm of the chair. A glass rolls slowly off corner of desk & smashes on the floor. Pause. The right hand of the dead man slips from the desk & swings limp to a standstill. Pause. A coal falls out of the fire Pause.

There is a blow at the door, & Arthur Norris bursts into the room. A smallish man of 35; well dressed, very white, nervous & excited keeps his hat on & flourishes stick. The occupant of the chair cannot be seen from the door, except his arms.

Norris (<u>looking round room</u>): Ah! You're here Lethaby & she isn't! Look here, I've got to talk to you, Lethaby. You're expecting my wife.

Walks downstage & begins what is evidently to a certain extent a premeditated speech, accusing Lethaby of "carrying on" with Mrs. Norris, saying that he has suspected it for some time etc, & that he chanced to see a telegram addressed to her from Lethaby fixing a rendezvous for that afternoon. And so he has come to surprise them & has got there first.

He stops suddenly in middle of speech, struck by impassive stillness of Lethaby in the chair.

Approaches and discovers that Lethaby is dead. "Lethaby!" he exclaims, & then: "Dead"! He is tremendously stressed.

"What was I talking about?" he asks himself. "What must I do? Call someone I suppose?"

There is a telephone on desk. It rings. Pause. Telephone rings again. At length Norris takes up the telephone.

"What is it? Who? Who's coming up? Mrs. Norris? Do you say Mrs. Norris?" Drops telephone. "Good God!!"

Then he says as if suddenly recollecting the facts:

"Of course she was coming to see him! Of course she's keeping the rendezvous. She'll see it! No, she mustn't see it, she mustn't."

He begins to push the big chair up stage. Then he surrounds it with the draught screen, hiding the chair & the corpse completely.

Enter Mrs. Norris. She wears a cloak over evening dress. She comes in with a certain air of confidence & stops short at sight of her husband. Silence.

Norris: So this is how you go your short cut from Adelphi Terrace to the Grand Babylon Hotel, - through the City? Before going to your precious dinner with Stanway & the Folkards you came to see your lover! etc. You thought I didn't see that wire. Well, I did. And I've caught you.

She asseverates she has come on business only.

A great row scene between them, in which she is roundly accused of unfaithfulness, & all the secret bitterness of their married life during recent weeks comes out.

She ends it by saying: "Well if you're going into mock heroics I'll leave you. It's clear I can't see Mr. Lethaby though I was told he was here."

Norris. He is here & you can see him.

He rushes to screen & pulls it aside, exposing the chair. But she has gone. His afterthought "It's just as well she didn't see it" (for he is fundamentally a humane man).

She has left door wide open, with its outer face to the audience. On this outer face is an 'In and Out' board, with In now shown. The door gives on a public passage in a sort of 'Manchester House' building. Opposite, on the other side of the passage, is a ground-glass door, illuminated from behind, with name in black letters showing "William Stanway".

Norris shuts door furiously & partly replaces the screen. He is thinking out the situation.

"Lies! Lies! Lies!" he says.

Looks at corpse; takes off his hat.

"Someone's killed him. It might have been me! Suppose they say it is me? By Jove!"

His manner alters as he perceives his danger & the necessity of escaping. Collects his hat, gloves, stick etc & goes to door.

Returns under some morbid necessity, of adjusting the room & replacing screen. Telephone rings & rings, but he is quite oblivious of it.

Then a knock at the door.

He nervously rushes to door & locks it.

"No! no!" he says. "This wont do!" "A letter for you to sign, sir," says a voice outside.

He opens door. Enter Paterson, Lethaby's aged clerk.

"Oh! It's Mr. Norris. I didn't know you were here, sir," says Paterson. Nervous remark from Norris, attempting to explain shutting of door.

Paterson: Isn't Mr. Lethaby here, sir?

Norris: Doesn't look like it! I just looked in, haven't any time now! I'm going to a dinner where I am not expected. Just time to dress; that's all."

Exit Norris in a high state of excitement leaving door open.

Paterson (shortsighted) advances to table & lays letter down. Then he goes to door & alters 'In' to 'Out'. He gradually perceives that the room is thoroughly disarranged. (Mr. Norris in his hysteric efforts to arrange it, has got everything wrong).

Paterson: "Where's the screen, then?"

Stanway appears through his doorway on the opposite side of the passage. He is in evening dress with overcoat, silk hat etc. He is a strong, determined, calm, dark-complexioned man. He hesitates & then comes into Lethaby's office.

Stanway: "Anything amiss, Paterson?

Paterson: No, sir, only Mr. Lethaby's gone out without telling me, & left his room in a fine mess. Now this screen __

He removes screen.

Disclosure of corpse.

Stanway (calmly after a pause) He is here after all! Great sensation again. Paterson says Norris has just left & then he begins to lament the loss of his situation at his age etc. Stanway comforts him & promises him a situation. Stanway picks up a cigarette case that is on table, Paterson watching him.

Paterson: That's not Mr. Lethaby's cigarette case.

Stanway: (handing it to Paterson) No, I don't think it is. You'd better take care that nothing is moved. Keep everything. Leave everything & go & tell the police. Pause. He continues "It's rather inconvenient this is. You say Mr. Norris has been here. I know Mr. Norris very well & Mrs. Norris is dining with me tonight. I don't want my name to be brought into the affair. He gets keener in this idea, & suggests that there is no reason why Paterson should say that he has looked into the room - at any rate for the present, as if it was known, it would make his presence at the dinner impossible.

Exit Stanway.

Paterson (despairingly) Don't leave me here all alone, sir."

Curtain

● ● ● ● ● ● ● ● ● ● ● ● ●

Act II

Private Dining Room at Grand Babylon Hotel

Time. same evening. 7.30 pm.

The occasion is a dinner given by Stanway to Mr. Folkard M.P. & Mrs. Folkard, their daughter Annie: their nephew Frank Micheldever, & Mrs. Norris. Norris had been invited but had refused to come, owing to growing coolness between himself & his wife.

Exact business with maitre d'hotel, waiters etc.

Stanway, who ought of course to have been there first is late.

Enter fat & fussy Folkard M.P.

Then Mrs. Folkard.

Folkard. Isn't Annie with you?

Mrs. F. She's just coming.

Folkard. I saw young Frank in the vestibule, I think. I suppose those two are chattering together. I wont have it.

The situation is that both Stanway & F. Micheldever are in love with Annie. Folkard M.P. favours Stanway, as a man rising rapidly in the city & having enterprises in corporations with the great millionaire financier, Lethaby. Mrs. Folkard favours Frank. The real truth (which no-one knows except Frank & Annie & Mrs. Norris) is that Frank & Annie are secretly engaged (the audience do not know this till 3rd Act)

The talk between Mr. & Mrs. Folkard passes to the question of the Norris ménage. Mrs. F. believes in Mrs. Norris's complete innocence. Folkard M.P. is clumsily cynical about women.

Enter Annie & Micheldever together.

Folkard displeased at this sign of intimacy, but Annie firmly laughs it off. Folkard says something to show that he knows Micheldever to be rather in a mess in the city.

Enter Mrs. Norris affecting to be gay.

Then Stanway, perfectly calm, and properly apologetic for his lateness, which he explains by simply saying that he was detained. Stanway is thinking so much of his general demeanour, that he forgets his usual special deference to Annie. She notices this. He then notices it too, & overdoes his attentions. She shows that she is accustomed to interesting him. She watches Stanway inimically.

Then dinner & chatter.

Folkard M.P. takes the lead. He is very talkative on the subject of his health - particularly his heart.

A tactless reference to the absence of Norris is smoothed over by Stanway. Suddenly Norris appears in a tragic pose, in the doorway. He is in evening dress but rather dishevelled.

"So Norris has come after all!" says Folkard M.P. rising from his seat & catching Norris a slap on his back which impels him violently into the room. Norris's carefully prepared tragic pose collapses. He sits down to table (extra cover put for him - business of maitre d'hotel etc) & complains of being hot & asks for the window to be opened. It is opened. In the meantime he makes three separate attempts to tell his wife publicly of the murder of Lethaby & fails, being each time suppressed by the pompous facetiousness of Folkard M.P. Stanway is cool but watchful.

The sound of a boy crying papers is heard through the open window, at first faintly, then more loud, but never louder than is necessary for the hearing of the words by the audience.

"Murder! Horrible murder! Murder in the city! Horrible Murder! Murder! Murder! Horrible murder in the city! Murder! Murder!

"Shut the window" says Stanway to a waiter. The waiter cannot at first persuade the window to fall & the sound of the boy's voice continues to be heard.

"Shut the window" rather hysterically from Stanway.

"Why that's only life!" says Folkard M.P. "That's only life that is. An everyday incident! What's a murder more or less? You look startled Norris! Never heard of a murder before? Still we'll have a look at the thing. Waiter, send for a paper." Exit waiter. "That reminds me of a story," Folkard M.P. goes on. And begins a long complicated tedious yarn; he is still telling it when the waiter returns with the paper. He motions to the waiter to put the paper on a side table. Stanway half rises to get the paper, but Folkard M.P. says "Presently, presently! As I was saying," And proceeds with his yarn. Micheldeve, not disguising that Folkard's story bores him, reaches out for the paper, which he can take without getting up from his chair & begins to read it.

"By Jove!" he exclaims.

"Stop!" cries Norris, jumping up in a state of high excitement.

"Stop! don't trouble to read it, Frank! I'll tell them! Lethaby has been murdered in his office, scarcely two hours ago!" He gazes wildly at his wife & continues "Yes, he was dead when you were there Lilian! I - I came here in order to tell you!

"How did you know?" asks Stanway, amid an awful silence.

"I was there" cries Norris. "I've just come from there. I only called at the flat for a b & s, & to change. Thought I'd break it to you decently. Oh, yes. He's dead right enough. Here! give me the damned paper & I'll see if they've got it right."

Snatches paper & reads aloud. "Stop press news etc. "Yes that's right!" Then to his wife, "Now you know. Didn't you notice the screen? Well, his corpse was behind it!"

Terrific scene between them.

Norris implies that he himself killed Lethaby, but he will not say so outright at first.

"You!"

"Who else? who had a better right than I?"

Mrs. Norris: "Leave me with him for a few moments, will you? He doesn't know what he's saying, Arthur-"

No one goes. But directly she begins to reason with her husband, he breaks out again & brings a great wealth of circumstantial detail to prove his guilt.

"And now I'm going to the police station." he says.

"What for?"

"To give myself up."

Attempts to stop him from leaving by several people. Folkard M.P. has what he considers to be a heart attack. And during the rumpus Norris escapes.

Stanway takes charge of the situation. He & Micheldever go after Norris, and asks Mrs. Folkard to look after Mrs. Norris & take her home. Mrs. Folkard, however, is busy with her fat husband (no one else takes the slightest notice of the fat husband & his heart attack.

Annie Folkard quietly steps forward & says, "I will look after Mrs. Norris." Lines of mutual admiration between Stanway & Annie for their cool self-restraint, kindred spirits etc! So thinks Stanway.

Curtain

• • • • • • • • • • • • •

Act III

Room at Norris' flat

Time, same evening, clock striking eleven.

Annie discovered standing in front of fire.

A servant enters & says that Stanway is come & wants to see Mrs. Norris (who is trying to regain calm in her bed room).

"What am I to do"? asks servant.

Annie. "I'll see him."

Enter Stanway.

Scene between Stanway & Annie.

Each recounts what he or she has done. Stanway has caused Norris to be searched for in vain. Annie has brought Mrs. Norris home & looked after her. A reference by Stanway to Folkard's seizure only makes Annie smile. They are both calm & equal to the situation, & they admire each other for this calmness.

Suddenly Stanway breaks out into passionate exclamations of his love for Annie.

Annie (moved). You mustn't talk in that strain now!

Stanway. Why not?

Annie. While we're in this awful crisis!

Stanway. Crisis! You are the crisis for me!

She is astounded by the revelation of the depth of his feeling.

She weeps.

Annie. I'm very sorry. I'd no idea you felt like this. I thought you were paying court to me simply as part of your scheme for getting on in the world. I'll tell you something that no one else knows. Frank Micheldever & I are secretly engaged.

Stanway (overcome) You - to him! But he isn't at all like you!

Annie. I know. But I'm the sort of woman he wants. What use should I be to a man like you! We both have the same qualities, we shouldn't complete each other. Etc

He is overcome. He tries to behave as he feels: but he merely enlarges & makes a fool of himself. Annie finding she cannot stand the strain any longer, says she will go & see if Mrs. Norris is better. Exit Annie.

Stanway (alone) By God! I can do everything, except these human things. Why couldn't I show my feelings more when she chucked me? I did feel. etc. Well, it's domino with me now.

Enter Mrs. Norris.

Big scene between her & Stanway.

She tells him the whole history of her relations with Lethaby. Quite innocent, though she liked Lethaby. Doesn't spare her-self. She explains that the real reason of her recent visits to Lethaby was that she wished to persuade him to help Frank Micheldever, who was in a mess. She knew of the secret engagement & wanted to help the young people. She implores him to do his best to stop her husband from making a fool of himself. Is sure that he has only accused himself out of jealous pride [This is true] Says she knew her husband to his marrow & loves him. Etc.

Paterson, Lethaby's old servant is shown in. He doesn't see Mrs. Norris. He is very old, feeble, blind etc.

Paterson (to Stanway) The police have been. I've been looking for you all over London, Mr. Stanway. You've promised to give me a situation & I don't want to do anything to annoy you: but I shall have to tell the police that you just looked in to the office after the murder. They want to know everything. I know it'll be very awkward for you to have to give evidence against Mr. Norris, but I daresay you'll have to - in a way, not direct like, but -

Mrs. Norris perceives in a flash that Stanway must have known of the murder all through the dinner & must have been acting his surprise when Norris burst out.

Stanway tries to stop Paterson, but Paterson being deaf, mis-understands him & keeps on.

Paterson. And about this cigarette case, sir. You told me to put it back on the desk & I put it in my pocket, & I've been carrying it about ever since. What am I to do?

Stanway takes cigarette case & dismisses Paterson.

Great scene between Mrs. Norris & Stanway.

She corners him on the point of his acting at the dinner. He admits it, & gives a plausible explanation of the advisability of concealment at the dinner.

Mrs. Norris. And that's your cigarette case.

Stanway. Yes.

Mrs. Norris. And was it on Lethaby's desk?

Stanway (calmly) That cigarette case was my grand error.

Stanway's great confession scene, in which he states his philosophy of life. He killed Lethaby, because Lethaby wouldn't agree not to help Frank Micheldever. He has no moral scruples (sort of superman) Now all has failed through cigarette case.

Mrs. Norris. Would you have let my husband hang, if he had insisted on pretending that he was the murderer?

Stanway. Not now! I could have done before! But I changed my mind ten minutes ago.

Mrs. Norris: Why?

Stanway. Because ten minutes ago I learnt there was no chance for me with Annie Lethaby. I loved her. I love her.

Enter Norris, who through vacillation has been unable to make up his mind to give himself up.

The play ends with a very tender scene of reconciliation & mutual comprehension between Norris & his wife.

During this scene Stanway slips away to surrender himself to the police.

Curtain

●●●●●●●●●●●●●●

Bennett's thoughts on how the play should be staged are interesting in their own right. He clearly has a notion of breaking from established norms of contemporary popular theatre by observing a strict classic French dramatic unity of time and action in order to foster a greater sense of reality. This reality would be augmented by the novel suggestion of dispensing with scenic curtains in a West End theatre. Bennett's introductory 'Note' on creating a psychological drama that grips the 'tense interest of the audience from the outset, so as to keep 'them tightly strung up till the final scene', reads as the storyboard for an Alfred Hitchcock film, along the lines of, say, *Rear Window* (1954).

Observant Bennett readers will have noticed that Bennett sets Act II in the Grand Babylon Hotel, returning to the scene of rather more sensational international crimes depicted in his recent popular and commercial fictional success.

Marriott's watercolour of the view from Bennett's Trinity Hall farmhouse

29. PARIS

It was his habit to read while having his breakfast. He used to prop up the book or paper against the sugar basin or some other convenient piece of pottery.

One morning, he suddenly looked up from the Balzac he was reading, and turning to me said, 'I shall go to live in Paris when I am thirty'. It didn't transpire what had caused him so unexpectedly to make that resolve; perhaps something in the book he was reading, or, maybe the idea had occurred to him in the night, during one of his wakeful periods. Already he was known to be a poor sleeper, and at times he worried about it. He seldom confessed to having had a really good night's rest.

He did in fact fulfil his resolve and went to live in Paris at about the age of thirty, and he regularly contributed to English newspapers and periodicals, which provided him with an income while he established himself as a novelist and playwright. He rented a flat in the Rue de Douai, and while he was there, we decided to spend our Easter holidays in Paris, and it was our first continental experience.

The Channel boats of those days were very different in both size and comfort from those of today, and we arrived in Paris feeling very sorry for ourselves, after a particularly rough crossing. However, after we had made good the waste by a good square meal, and had been further refreshed by sleep, we soon forgot our distressing adventure in the English Channel and could even look back on it with amusement. How fortunate it is that the memory of the nauseating sensations of sea-sickness so quickly wear off, and become material for jest.

The next morning I got up at six o'clock, and went out before breakfast to seek out the street in which Bennett lived, and was pleased to find that it was within easy walking distance of our hotel.

After breakfast we went round to his flat, and found him preparing to go out for his morning walk. He said that he should be working all morning, but would spend the afternoon and evening with us. He asked where we would like to go, and I said to the Luxembourg. It was arranged that we should call for him at around noon, and then go together to a Cafe for lunch.

He took us to a cafe in a small side street which seemed to be patronised principally by budding young painters and musicians; young men who wore their hair a generous length; 'wide-a-wake' hats, velvet jackets and 'peg top' corduroy trousers, soft collars, and a plentiful display of cravat.

The food and cooking were excellent and abundant, and a small decanter of vin ordinaire was, to our great surprise served free to each person. During the progress of the meal, classical music was discoursed by a quartet of string instruments played by students from a conservatoire of music nearby. Bennett told us that three considerations attracted him to that cafe; the excellence of the cooking and music, and the moderate charges. He introduced us to several similar places during our stay.

We went on to the Luxembourg Gallery which was fairly near. It is perhaps the most interesting store-house there is in the world of modern artistic experiment and achievement, both in painting and sculpture.

Bennett didn't talk much while we went through the rooms; he never did in public galleries, but I noticed that he went quickly past the very academic, historical subjects, and story-telling pictures, and lingered in front of such as displayed spontaneity, movement, freshness of vision and technique. He had a passionate love for both art and music, and while he had a keen appreciation of the old masters, the most modern and experimental movements excited his interest also.

In the sculpture gallery, the work of Rodin claimed his closest attention, for at that time the work of Rodin was a very controversial subject, and opinions for and against it were very sharply divided. He had no time for art which was dull, commonplace and hackneyed.

****

RESTORED TEXT

Then we spent some time in the Luxemburg gardens, the most delightful of playgrounds for the children of Paris, and where mothers and nursemaids sit knitting, sewing and gossiping with their work-bags beside them, while the more aged people rest and meditate, or read books and newspapers. The French, and indeed all the continental peoples make much more of their open spaces and public gardens than we do in England.

The liberal display of sculpture displayed over various parts of the gardens looked like an overflow from the gallery, and certainly it would have been difficult to find a better setting for the specimens.

****

One afternoon he took us along the embankment of the Seine to the long line of dusty picturesque book stalls which occupy portions of the quays, where one could rummage at will among the miscellaneous collections which constitute the book-seller's stocks. We passed from stall to stall without being pestered in any way to buy, while the owners sat smoking or reading their newspapers. Bennett told us of book bargains he had picked up there at odd times, but he said that he had on occasion got rarer bargains in the Farringdon Road and the East End of London.

On the bank of the river below, Bennett pointed out a poodle being shorn in the fantastic fashion of French poodles. The operation was performed by a bearded old man, while his wife held the dog, keeping it more-or-less quiet by means of small pieces of biscuit, and close by on the brink of the river sat one of the many melancholy anglers who frequent the banks of the Seine, quite unperturbed by the agitations of the dog.

Indeed, as far as the eye could see both up and down the river, the edge of the water seemed to be lined with these imperturbable fishermen, who were oblivious to all external happenings; surely they must be the calmest and most patient units of the city which has the reputation of being the gayest city in the world.

Across ocean and channel Art calls hosts of young painters who inhabit mysterious three roomed studio flats in Paris, and who live delightfully care-free by the help of regular funds from their homes. It is a remarkable thing, that these people could get to work regularly by eight o'clock in the morning in Julian's Studio in Paris, though it had been difficult for them to get to work by ten o'clock in the schools they had left in England and America.

Bennett's disposition for sociability, combined with his intense interest in art and music, caused him to make many friends following these professions, and he was a frequent visitor to their studios; consequently he was able to introduce us to the holders of some of the Parisian studio flats.

To visit these rising artists involved climbing narrow staircases to the top floors of the buildings, where tea was served amidst the disordered jumble of studio properties, and studies for pictures in varying stages of progress. Without doubt, the fortunate people who are able to follow art as a profession can get more joy out of life on slender means than those of any other profession.

30. A MOVEABLE FEAST

Bennett's first visit to Paris was from 23 to 31 October 1897 in the company of his friend Edwin Rickards. Unlike the cheerful Marriott, Rickards may not have been the ideal companion for an initiation into the attractions of this most fun-loving of cities. His tendency towards talking into the early hours of the morning about architecture, coupled with his somewhat gloomy outlook on life may have contributed to a sense of fatigue and disillusionment that colours Bennett's *Journal* entries for the period.

Things begin in typical Bennett fashion with the two friends wasting no time in sampling the cultural night-life of Paris: 'On my first evening in Paris it was proper that I should see *Faust* at the Opèra'.[108] Again, with typical punctilious Bennett time-keeping, they took their seats some 20 minutes before the curtain rose, finding themselves in 'a vast interior honeycombed with corridors in which people, by comparison insignificant as ants, were rushing wildly about, arguing, gesticulating, and quarrelling with the harpy like ouvreuses'.[109] There was a sense of rapt excitement in the audience which would have conveyed itself to Bennett, who left the theatre caught up in the excitement greeting the serial publication of Zola's *Paris*. And yet, 24 hours later and Bennett, normally so quick to identify a sense of place and the psychology of a people writes that 'I search for the formula which would express Paris -- in vain'.[110] Whatever Bennett's own reservations, his powers of observation in making quick pen sketches of those around him remained intact. Having set the scene, Bennett proceeds to describe the people with the quickness of an artist's sketch:

Nursemaids, whose large white or blue aprons and white caps seem to strike the note of the scene; scores of children, many just able to walk, others learning to skip or clumsily trundling hoops, others in arms; the last seemed always to be receiving clean napkins from their plump, comfortable nurses.

Students in fine black hats and vast neckties, walking about or sitting in groups.

The Chairwoman, a buxom young woman, capless, with a large black apron. She goes to a group of young students who are talking and laughing among themselves. Without apparently noticing her, they throw her a few words, still laughing, a colloquy ensues, and then for some reason she goes away without exacting pennies from them.

Young women, carelessly *chic*, some powered, all talkative, sitting about in pairs, with looks on their faces of invitation.

Here and there a few sedater groups, well dressed; *papa, mama et bebé,* or perhaps several old women full of volubility and gesture.

A few inquisitive dogs.[111]

But Bennett is not satisfied, recording in the same entry that he 'has periods of gloom', suspecting that 'he is not seeing the right things', and that details of 'strange scenes' elude him.

Nothing that happens over the course of the next few days does anything to dispel Bennett's unusual loss of self-confidence. Here is Bennett on the verge of his career as a novelist but wracked by doubts:

He [Bennett] has periods of gloom, periods when he asks himself the object of all these exertions ... At such times he suspects that he is not seeing the right things... He is disgusted because his money is not more, his command of the language so slight, and his capacity for enjoyment so limited. His mind goes forward to speculate as to his future career, which seems one of but narrow possibilities, and he foresees failure.[112]

Posterity has inherited a general picture of Bennett as a self-assured, almost arrogant, figure who had his life mapped out from an early period. It is too easy to forget that it was only four years before this Paris visit that he had summoned the nerve to abandon his legal career; in the 1890s he owed his editorship of *Woman* to money from his father; he remained largely dependent on a fluctuating income from serial sales to keep him afloat in the style to which he aspired; several of his early short stories involve struggling artists; the shoulder-chip of being a provincial among cosmopolitans was never far away. It was not until Bennett put his affairs in the hands of the literary agent J. B. Pinker, in 1901, that he could rely on a steady income, albeit one necessarily augmented by monetary advances.

The restored section of Marriott's memoir shows a Luxembourg Gardens and its habitués little changed from when Bennett first visited and recorded his impressions - what has changed is Bennett, confident in his powers, on the cusp of becoming a celebrity, and one of England's highest paid writers. This is the Bennett we encounter in Marriott's next chapter.

31. LES SABLONS

Marriott etching: *Courtyard in Moret*:
'The charm of Moret irresistibly compels all artists who go there to work.'

In the Spring of 1907, it had been arranged that my wife and I should spend a month in the Summer with Arnold Bennett at Les Sablons where he was then living.

The week before we were due to go we received the unexpected news that he had embarked on a matrimonial enterprise, and we naturally thought this event would upset our plans.

I wrote to him at once, suggesting that in consequence of his recent marriage he might like us to put off our visit till a later date. His reply, written on a post card, was characteristically brief. It read, 'Dear Frederick, I shall need you all the more. A.B.' Thus it came about that we spent one of the most delightful holidays possible, and were introduced to a very beautiful and romantic region of France only forty miles distant from Paris.

On our arrival at Moret (the nearest station to Les Sablons) we found our host waiting on the station platform, and he quickly transferred us and our luggage to a cab. While we were driving to Les Sablons, he told us that his wife could only speak a few words of English, and that we should have to make the most of our few words of French.

When the cab drew up to the door of the house, Mrs. Bennett met us radiant and smiling, and with a short halt between each word, said, 'How do you do, will you take tea with me?', an opening evidently previously rehearsed. Our subsequent interchange of broken English and broken French, supported by expressive gesticulations to cover our deficiencies, was productive of much merriment between us during our time there, and on many other occasions. She was a tall, graceful, and strikingly handsome woman, and she had excellent taste in dress. Moreover, she had the gift of wearing fine clothes with the best effect.

Bennett rented the greater part of the house which belonged to a retired government official, whose chief activity was attending to the garden which he kept in perfect order, and which was well stocked with fruit, flowers, and vegetables; more than sufficient for the household requirements.

From the point of view of picturesqueness we found Les Sablons unworthy of its setting. It consists of a number of featureless dwelling houses lining both sides of a small portion of the main road running from Moret to Fontainebleau; but there are beautiful gardens, and it possesses the desirable advantage of quietude. Being situated about a mile and a quarter from the ancient town of Moret, and close to the edge of the Forest of Fontainebleau, it was an ideal spot for either writers or artists, but Bennett was the only representative of these professions living in the village.

Moret, however, was very different in this respect, for the town was besieged by every type of amateur and professional artist; owing to its easy accessibility from Paris, and to the wealth of subject material which the town and surrounding country provided for both painters and etchers.

It is picturesquely placed on the bank of the river Seine, possesses two imposing turreted gateways; one at each end of the main street. When Bennett first took me through the town, I was thrilled by the pictorial possibilities it offered, and I lost no time before investigating every corner of it, under varying conditions of lighting both by day and night.

The charm of Moret irresistibly compels all artists who go there to work, even in face of the knowledge that its beauties have been so admirably portrayed by Sisley and other great painters; so this knowledge didn't deter me from compiling such a number of drawings and colour sketches that they served me with material for etchings and paintings for a considerable time afterwards.

At intervals, Bennett and I explored on our cycles most of the towns and villages within a radius of thirty miles. And what a fascinating district for cycling in; so closely packed with interest everywhere. It was doubly interesting to traverse it under the guidance of a man with such remarkable powers of observation and analysis. Never have I met anyone possessing a keener faculty for quickly selecting and absorbing the essential architectural features and characteristics of towns and countryside, or with a more reliable memory for storing impressions.

On one of the shining lustrous days common in France, I was thrilled when Bennett suggested that we should go together to Barbizon, a place made famous by that brilliant group of French painters known as the 'Barbizon School': Corot, Rousseau, Millet, Daubigny, Diaz, and Dupre.

I thought we should be making the excursion on our cycles, but to my surprise, at the appointed time, a motor car which Bennett had secretly ordered drove up to the door, so in addition to our objective, we were able to take a wider view of the country round about.

Architecturally the village of Barbizon was rather characterless and disappointing, save for the buildings containing the celebrated studios; but the forest and landscape near at hand was in every sense pictorial, and charged with an endless variety of intriguing and suggestive painting material.

While we wandered through the village, we discussed the work of the various members of the 'Barbizon School' and analyzed the characteristic differences in their outlook and treatment of their subjects. We marvelled that a group of great artists deriving their inspirations from the same surroundings should produce such divergent results; demonstrating how inexhaustible is the range of appeal and individuality of expression in art.

●●●●●●●●●●●●●●●●●

RESTORED TEXT

As we looked across this rich and undulating tract of country, we concluded that it would be extremely difficult to find any other colony of artists who had worked together, who differed more widely in outlook, colour, and technique.

For instance, the work of Corot, Rousseau, and Millet is as different as it well could be. Corot seemed to have been searching always for the silvery tones and atmospheric effects, silent pools, rustling and wind-blown trees sparkling with dewy moisture. Very intimate and tender.

Rousseau was attracted by the massive oaks of the district with their great spreading leafy arms. The forest glades, full of depth and mystery, and pierced with warm glowing sunset lights. Who can roam through the Forest of Fontainebleau without being pleasantly reminded of the landscapes of Rousseau?

Then there was Millet, whose interest was centred more on the peasant life of the neighbourhood, set against the background of simplified passages of landscape.

He invested the peasant worker with a monumental dignity which has never been surpassed. We talked of his 'Angelus' and were agreed, that although it was his most popular picture ,it was far from being one of his best works, and that it owed its popularity chiefly to sentiment. The 'Angelus' was sold in 1899 for the extraordinary sum of £22,000!

It is interesting to note what these great painters thought of each other's work. Corot said of Millet, 'His work is a strange country to me. I like my own little music better.'

Of Corot, Millet said, 'His pictures are very beautiful but show nothing new'.

Speaking of Daubigny, Corot said, 'I thank Heaven that I have lived in the same country as that great painter.'

It is generally conceded that the Barbizon group of painters strongly were influenced by that robust painter of English landscape, John Constable, who was then regularly exhibiting at the Paris Salon. It is true that Constable had brought a new vision to the art of landscape painting.

•••••••••••••

Bennett was very appreciative of the work of these painters, and had taken me to see the representative collection of their works at the Louvre when I visited him in Paris.

32. 'NEED YOU ALL THE MORE'

The suddenness of Bennett's marriage to Marguerite Souliè was of a piece with an earlier hasty engagement in the summer of 1906 to a young American, Eleanor Green, which lasted barely seven weeks. After his *Journal* entry on 3 August 1906 - 'At 11 a.m. on this day at Camel, my engagement to Eléanora was broken off'[113] - he made no further entries until 19 July 1907, sixteen days after his marriage to Marguerite. The engagement to Eleanor may have existed more in Bennett's mind than in reality. His slip of the pen when confiding in H.G.Wells that 'I am - I mean *we* are [italics added] - thinking of being married in a registry office in Folkestone'[114] should have given pause for thought. And the fanciful notion that a young lady of good family would be willing to forgo a lavish wedding ceremony lacks conviction: 'You will neither see nor hear anything of it. Eléanora will bring one friend over with her for a night, & the other witness I will get in the registry office'.[115] According to Bennett's biographer, Reginald Pound, who was given Eleanor's side of the relationship in a series of notes from the family:

> Although her family and friends knew that Bennett was in love with her, Miss Green never fully realised it herself, nor did she understand that he was completely serious when he proposed to her... She liked him, considered him 'nice enough'... [but] she never at any time thought of him in terms of the affections. He seemed to her always middle-aged and avuncular.[116]

To further confuse matters there exists a memoir by Eleanor's younger sister Anne, *With Much Love*, referred to by James Hepburn, which suggests that whilst Eleanor is not entirely indifferent, she is also caught up in events spiralling out of her control:

> 'Let me try to get used to him a little longer Mamma. He'll be broken-hearted if I fail him just as he's looking for an apartment.' So things go, and Eleanor is secretly interested in someone else, and eventually decides that she must make the break, after her mother refuses to do it for her. Fortunately Bennett is suspicious of her behaviour, and one day when they are holidaying together, she comes upon him examining the contents of her handbag. 'Uneasy Eleanor pounced on this occasion to be furious ...; she ... broke the engagement.'[117]

Whatever the truth of the matter, Bennett was clearly left distressed and in need of distraction. Writing to his friend, the music critic Michel Dimitri Calvocoressi from a holiday hotel in San Remo in early 1907, he expresses a wish to travel more but laments: 'If only I had people to travel with!'[118] Failing travel he thinks 'that an erotic club is needed down here'.[119] But Calvocoressi has already set in motion a new path for Bennett, one that initially promises a travelling companion who may also bring some erotic excitement into his life, by introducing him to Marguerite Soulié.

With Bennett's letters and journal silent on his courting of Marguerite, biographers have to rely on the veracity of Georges Lafourcade's account in his 1939 *Arnold Bennett: A Study*:

In January 1907 Arnold Bennett who was looking for a part-time secretary ... was introduced to Marguerite Soulié by his friend Calvocoressi. He at once accepted her services. [She] had come to Paris to live with an aunt who had offered her a respectable post in the 'maison de haute couture' which she superintended. But her interests were chiefly in the direction of dramatic art and she availed herself of her residence in Paris to take courses in elocution. She could recite French poetry with distinction and originality and had appeared on several stages. When she met Arnold Bennett she had just returned from a prolonged stay in England where her aunt had advised her to go to learn the language. Her knowledge of English made her services doubly acceptable. Bennett was attracted by her good presence and striking personality. On his return from a two months stay in Italy in the spring, she nursed him through a brief but violent illness in his bachelor's flat. He thus had occasion to note her remarkable qualities as a housewife and organizer of a home... In the course of May they were engaged and their wedding took place on July 4, 1907, at the Marie du IXe Arrondissement.[120]

An exception to Bennett's reticence on the subject of his engagement to Marguerite comes in a brief exchange of letters with H.G. Wells. Wells writes in June, 'So you *will* marry! Well, I've warned you once'. Bennett's reply, sent just three days before the wedding, ignores the only half-in-jest warning whilst nevertheless sounding an ominous note: 'I had to come back to Paris by telegram, to arrange legal formalities for the accursed union. No end of trouble'.[121] And indeed no end of trouble was in store, as could have been inferred from Bennett's wish for the Marriott's visit to go ahead when convention, common sense, and sexual pleasure might have prescribed a private honeymoon period for the couple.

Early signs of the arguments to come, and the eventual rift in the marriage, are apparent in a frankly confessional letter of 29 July to his sister Tertia supposedly reporting on the Marriott's stay, but very easily decoded from its opening as the cry of a man who already knows he has made a calamitous life-mistake. It begins: 'The only worm gnawing at the root of my mind is that this business of being married cannot possibly last as it is.

It can last perfectly well on my footing; but it cannot last on her footing'.[122] And yet, beyond this deeply ingrained Victorian patriarchal attitude there is a sense of pride in his wife that comes out when he talks of the Marriott's impressions of her:

> I am about a century older than my wife, though she is 32, and has been through pretty considerable things in the way of misfortune. Marriott put her age at 26, & Mrs. Marriott at 28. The fact is that she looked her age six months ago, but has steadily been getting younger during the last three months. So far as I can judge Marriotts are somewhat taken with her. He said to me in his serious solemn tone, with that peculiar look which he can't help wearing at such moments: 'Bennett, your wife is a beautiful woman.'... M. considers Mrs. Marriott better dressed than most Englishwomen, but she objects to her jewels. So do I. There is too much Frederick about them.[123]

Bennett was so overcome with excitement over the Marriott's visit that he failed to masticate his dinner in his customary slow fashion, with the inevitable result in his case that he suffered from indigestion. He already knew Marriott's wife, Margaret Hannah, known familiarly as Tully, very well from the seven years he had lived with them in Chelsea .The closeness of their friendship is further cemented when they asked Bennett in 1911 to be godfather to their adopted daughter, Menetta, born to one of Frederick's sisters in Australia. Menetta's adoption was to find an uncanny but far less happy parallel when in 1916, and largely at Marguerite's instigation, she and Arnold unofficially adopted Richard, the eldest son of Bennett's brother Frank. Marguerite may have longed to replicate the success of the Marriott's adoption, but with Richard at the rebellious age of 16 at the time he came to live with them in Essex, and with his uncle often absent in London on war work, Marguerite's strict temperament meant a failure to bond with him. (Dudley Barker's biography of Bennett has a comprehensive chapter on 'Adopting Richard'.[124])

Bennett's letter to his sister goes on to say that the 'Marriotts are good visitors. The conversation is extremely intimate, but of course you can't talk to Frederick *really* about human nature. He would get frightened. I don't think Tully would; but he would. So we keep off IT'. Then, a few lines later he gives the reader reason to doubt his own understanding of human nature, especially where marriage is concerned. He contrasts his insomnia with Marguerite's ability to 'sleep like two logs - but not in *my* room. The one difficulty that I have in marriage is to refrain from looking after everything. I am so used to controlling every department of my household, from washing to dusting, that I continually forget that it is no longer necessary for me to worry about things'.[125] But worry he does about every domestic detail, leaving Marguerite with little room to use her own initiative or to pursue her artistic career with any confidence. In this respect Marriott could have taught Bennett a few truths about human nature.

Perhaps Bennett should have given greater attention to the two beautifully intimate crayon portraits of Marguerite that Marriott sketched during his stay at Les Sablons. These show a woman deserving of his attention and, equally importantly, his understanding of her difficult social position amongst his many friends and associates of whom she knew so little. We have access to very few contemporary portraits by Marriott, and these two along with his portrait of Bennett done at the same time, are testament to his ability to capture the essence of a personality in a few deft strokes.

Marriott's sketch of Marguerite at Les Sablons.

Marriott's portrait of Frank Clayton Bennett, father of the unofficially adopted Richard.

(Potteries Museum & Art Gallery)

33. FONTAINEBLEAU

It was under the guidance of Arnold Bennett that I first entered the great Forest of Fontainebleau, perhaps the most enchanting and richly wooded region in France, within such easy reach from Paris.

It differed from any other forest of my experience, in that it bristled with innumerable directional sign posts. The forest was intersected by a number of wide main roads for vehicular traffic, with narrow foot paths branching off them in every direction. There was a sign post at the junction of every foot path with the main road, and at every point where one path crossed another there was a sign post. Moreover, at each of the main road entrances there was a large conspicuous notice board, bearing general rules and instructions relating to the sign posts.

The necessity for the multiplicity of guide signs were soon explained when we began wandering along the winding side-tracks into the dense growths, for without them it would be a very easy matter to get lost for hours. While we walked, Bennett told me that he intended writing a novel which would have the forest and the town of Fontainebleau as the background, but it never matured.

The great variety of trees and undergrowths were so thickly planted in many parts of the forest, that they presented a mysterious and almost impenetrable appearance.

Scattered about the open spaces, and mixed up with the undergrowth there were immense crops of great grey boulders, some of them of enormous size, which were covered with lovely golden and bronze-green mosses and patches of silvery lichen, very beautiful in colour. Many of these boulders resembled huge primitive sculptured animals, and were very impressive.

After wandering about for some time, we came upon that great residence of kings, the Palace of Fontainebleau; at one time the home of Napoleon the great, and now the fitting repository for many of the historical relics he left behind.

The richness of the Palace reflected the beauty and richness of the surrounding forest, which provided an appropriate setting for such a huge architectural display.

It is common knowledge that the Palace of Fontainebleau is the

Marriott's etching of Rue Gubernalis, Nice (Goldsmiths Art Collection)

most popular of the palaces of France, and being so accessible from Paris, it is always well supplied with tourists who are conducted through its salons in groups of about twenty at regular intervals every day of the week, under the domination of official guides.

Of course Bennett was already well acquainted with the Palace and its contents, and owing to his rooted objection to official guides, I had a difficulty in persuading him to tour the interior again.

On entering the building we found a party just commencing the round under the leadership of a guide, and we merged ourselves into the group, and were hurried through all the show rooms of the Palace in less than an hour!

As guides go, ours was well up to standard, but Bennett felt it was an affront to be compelled to follow in the wake of a chattering official, who was evidently working to a sort of time table, which left us no opportunity for the more leisurely examination of any particular specimens in which we were interested.

With very good reason, Bennett argued that there was no real necessity for these guides, and claimed that if a guardian were placed in charge of every two or three rooms, as is the case in many other treasure houses, visitors would be able to study properly the best exhibits, and ignore such as were trivial or offensive.

Most of the show places of all countries are overcrowded with exhibits, and the Palace of Fontainebleau is no exception, and one felt that a judicious weeding out might be undertaken with advantage to the general effect, especially as the rooms are decorated with painted ceilings, and carved and gilded enrichments.

From the time Bennett first went to live in Paris, he developed a fondness for the Empire style of furniture, and as opportunity occurred, he collected good examples of it, mostly at attractively small prices. He not only bought Empire furniture, but bric-a-brac, hangings, and rugs of that period also, so that his house in Fontainebleau was furnished throughout in the Empire style, which accounted for his keen interest in the superb craftsmanship displayed in the Empire furniture on view in the rooms of the Palace. He was at the time genuinely impressed by the marvellous technical accomplishment of the French craftsmen, and by the richness of their designs.

The lavish display of luxury on all sides was amazing, and everything exhibited was of museum-specimen rank, and invested with some historical association which supplied a special interest.

As we passed from room to room, we were convinced that only expert skaters would be able to get full enjoyment out of the show, for the floors were polished to a surface finish equal to that of the finest skating rink, and after we had floundered about on them for the best part of an hour, we were glad to feel a gritty gravel path under our feet once more; having duly anointed the outstretched hand of our guide with 'palm oil', and retrieved our sketching materials from the depository.

When we came out, we found the Palace front glowing with warm sunlight, and the whole facade reflected in a large sheet of water, presenting a most tempting subject for painting, so we immediately got to work, and spent the remainder of our time sketching. Indeed, the picturesque surroundings of the Palace compelled two return visits.

(Some twenty years later, when talking to Bennett about a sketching tour I had made of French chateaux, he told me he had again visited the Palace of Fontainebleau, and I found that he had materially changed his views regarding exhibits of Empire furniture shown there. He severely criticised them as glaring examples of excesses in both style and ornamentation, and he had formed a very low estimate of Napoleon's culture and taste, as evidenced by his preference for ornate excesses, which he said had only resulted in a display of sumptuous vulgarity.)

On the wider outskirts of the Forest of Fontainebleau, there are many beautiful typically French towns and villages which admirably fit into the landscape, and seem to have grown quite naturally out of it. Bennett knew them all well, and he took me to a number, including Nemours, Chateau-Landon, Montereau, Donnemarie, Provins and Larchant. Our excursions to these places on our cycles were full of interest, and we did a good number of water-colours together. In Larchant particularly, I found plenty of excellent subjects for etchings, and I returned there several times for the purpose of making the drawings from which I ultimately etched my plates.

34. INTO THE WOODS

Bennett began writing Part III of his acknowledged masterpiece *The Old Wives' Tale* at Villa des Neflièrs, Avon, on the edge of the Forest of Fontainebleau, on 8 October, 1907, having moved there from Les Sablons. Place and person seemed perfectly matched to create just that creative distancing conducive to writing an epic novel of bustling English provincial life far removed from the immediate surroundings of the vast majesty of an ancient French forest. Not that Bennett's creative genius was ever able to flourish without a set of near-rigid rules: 'Yesterday I began *'The Old Wives' Tale'*. I wrote 350 words yesterday afternoon and 900 this morning. I felt less self-conscious than I usually do in beginning a novel. In order to find a clear 3 hours for it every morning I have had to make a time-table, getting out of bed earlier and lunching later'.[126] No matter what the weather Bennett would walk in the forest - 'A landscape of soaked leaves and thick clouds and rain ... But I like it'[127] - thinking all the time of how best to write the next portion of his novel. This pattern of perambulatory mental improvisatory plotting was one practised from early days on the Thames embankment when thinking about the next episode of the 19 part episodic serial *The Grand Babylon Hotel* for *The Golden Penny* magazine between 2 February and 15 June 1901. When the Fontainebleau weather was kind the writing took flight: 'A magnificent October day. I walked 4 miles between 8.30 and 9.30, and then wrote 1,000 words of the novel'.[128]

By 8 August, 1908, Bennett was able to report that 'I have now written 15,000 words of the last part of the novel. I expect to finish on September 1st'.[129] The completed novel was published on 30 October, 1908. Today the Villa Les Nèfliers survives virtually unscathed. To celebrate its importance as a literary site the Arnold Bennett Society marked the 100th anniversary of the publication of *The Old Wives' Tale* with the unveiling on 11 October 2008 of a handsome plaque made in the very Middleport pottery featured as Henry Mynors's works in Bennett's *Anna of the Five Towns*.

Marriott enjoyed his time with Bennett at Les Nèfliers, venturing out whenever the weather allowed to paint and sketch together in the surrounding towns and villages. He makes particular reference to being repeatedly drawn to the picturesque attractions of the village of Larchant, and we are fortunate to have an image of one of his etchings of the village from this period.

Marriott's etching of Larchant

35. MUSICAL EVENING IN 1907

When in December 1907, Arnold Bennett brought his wife Marguerite over from France to London for the first time, we celebrated the event by making it the occasion for a special evening in my studio, to which we invited as many of his friends as could be squeezed into it, and an excellent entertainment was provided by the musical members of the fraternity who gathered in full force.

The name of Arnold Bennett was already well known in France, and he was the chosen companion of some of the most famous French authors and composers, and in view of these facts, and out of compliment to his French wife, carefully selected items from the works of French masters were introduced into the first and more serious part of the programme to give an appropriate flavour to the proceedings.

During the interval for refreshment, speeches of welcome and eulogy occurred as the spirit moved various members, and reference was made to Bennett's rapid rise to fame, and he was acclaimed as a triumphant figure in the literary world.

Then followed the variety entertainment, when Stanley Hazell and others gave 'turns' specially written for the occasion, combined with some of the old favourites.

The following parody on *Sally in our Alley* was specially written by Hazell for me to sing as a comic impersonation of a Drawing room Tenor

Arnold Bennett.
Air: Sally in our Alley.

1. Of all my pals who are so smart -
Although you may not ken it -
The master of the writer's art
Is Enoch Arnold Bennett.
He'll throw off thrilling Fantasias
Or Belles Lettres liter-ary:
He used to haunt the Fulham Road.
But now he lives in Parry.

2. When first our Arnold took to ink
It made us all feel gladder,
I'll now proceed to climb, said he,

The literary ladder;
But when at last he reached the top
He found Hall Caine and Mahree -
He said 'Oh! .... I cannot stop'.
And so he went to Pahree.

3. Of all the days in the week
There's one day which is my day-
And that's a day that comes between
A Monday and a Friday:
I buy a, ha'penny paper, and
I find a 'Cure for worry'
For in the 'News' I can peruse
Philosophy from Purry.

4. Quand Monsieur Bennett nous laissait
Il était presque garçon:
Il aimaittoujours la beauté -
Je vous le dis en passant -
Il cueillait une belle fleur de France
Pour deveinr son mari:
Elle est la chérie de son coeur,
Et elle demeure - à Paris.

14 December, 1907. Stanley Hazell.

36. RIGHT NOTES

Bennett's *Journal* entry for Sunday, 15 September 1907 makes only a brief reference to the previous evening's entertainment; 'Last night, reception and musical evening given in our honour here at Marriott's'. Whilst his sole comment on the musical offerings is an acidic dismissal of a popular song: 'Why "The Devout Lover", a conventional, rotten song, become utterly conventionalised and as hard as a pebble, a thing now accepted without examination'.[130] Composed by Maude Valèrie White, with words by Walter Herries Pollock, and first published in 1882, it became an overnight success in late-Victorian England. Derek Hyde's recent study, *New-found Voices: Women in Nineteenth-Century English Music*[131] regards White as one of the most out-standing women song-writers of the 1890s; a

Hyperion recording of 1993 refers to its 'marvellous melody' describing White as to 'be fully the equal of Quilter, Elgar or Delius as a song composer'. So, what were these abhorrent lyrics that followed an extended piano introduction? :

1. It is not mine to sing the stately grace,
The great soul beaming in my lady's face,
To write no sounding odes to me is given,
Where in her eyes outshine the stars of heaven.

2. Not mine in flowing melodies to tell
The thousand beauties that I know so well.
Not mine to serenade her every tress
And sit and sigh my love in idleness.

3. But mine it is to follow in her train,
Do her behests in pleasure or in pain.
Burn at her alter love's sweet frankincense
And worship her in distant reverence.[132]

Few today would argue with Bennett's dismissal of such a sentimental and ethereal courtly hymn to love, but is Bennett's discomfort linked to his own inability to pen blazons? Certainly, days before his marriage, he was telling Marguerite that if he 'could shower praises on you and make them sound natural, I would do so. But I can't. If I tried, I would do it badly.'[133] And when, just days after his marriage, he struggles to complete a poem on *A Love Affair*, its feminine anatomical markers are crudely and deliberately autochthonic. Bennett's woman emerges 'from a clod' with 'waist and bosom agreeably zoned - But a clod'. 'Wit she had none to amuse, / Knew not the trade of a wife'. In the final verse:

Weary, he called on his God:
'Quench me this woman I've kissed!'
Lo! In due course she returned to the clod.
She was missed.[134]

It is clear that the speaker is male and the misogynist message addressed to a male reader. There is a disturbing patriarchal dualism, absent from the *The Devout Lover*, in which men are permitted 'gales of desire' stirred by 'breath of that bosom', but only until sated and then ready to metaphorically bury the 'witless' creature. This is problematic to say the least - Bennett's woman is defined in narrow sexual terms, and we do have to wonder at his seeming inability to recognize just how much of his own sexual insecurity is being psychoanalytically exposed. Romance reduced to 'trade' after brief male centred sensuality has run its course was antithetical to *The Devout Lover*'s commitment and an early warning to Marguerite of their troubled relationship to come. Finally, the form of Bennett's poem with short lines and simple rhyme scheme is in structure at least no different from the despised White/Pollock lyric.

I think it best to draw a veil over all of Bennett's, admittedly limited, attempts at writing poetry[135] and instead remember him as the fun-loving party-goer who would accompany himself at the piano whilst unashamedly singing the simplistic *Sipping Cider through a Straw*, very much as depicted in Marriott's lively sketch of him at Les Sablons in those early days of marriage.

By permission of Keele University Li

Arnold Bennett from a sketch by Frederick Marriott at
Les Sablons. August 1907

37. CALLIGRAPHY

It sometimes happens, that a chance suggestion from interested relatives or friends, will result in a marked change in the aims and working methods of an artist; and such was more than once the case with Arnold Bennett,

The incidents which led to the development and achievement of the beautiful specimens of calligraphy to be seen in many of his more important manuscripts present illuminating illustration.

Soon after he went to live at Les Sablons, his sister Tertia and her husband William Kennerley went to spend a short holiday with him, and they were concerned to find that he had entirely given up tennis which had been his favourite exercise, and that, save for short intervals of cycling recreation, he had no diversion from the absorbing scheme of work he was following; and they insisted that he ought to adopt some form of hobby.

In this connection, the following extract from his journal is interesting. It is dated July 1907. 'My youngest sister and her husband had pointed out to me the dreadful fact that I had absolutely no hobby, no diversion. I had played no game for years, I collected nothing, seriously. I did nothing, except work. It was a genuine fact, which had most strangely escaped my attention. They told me that I ought to have a hobby. And I saw that to make my life conform to the everlasting principles of common sense I indeed must have a hobby. Their arguments were unanswerable. So I sought for a hobby, and at last hit on fine calligraphy and the illumination thereof in colours. Thus it was that I became interested in calligraphy.'

It seems strange that he elected to adopt a hobby which at best was only another form of his usual work.

He must have very soon decided on fine calligraphy as his hobby, for Kennerley possesses the first piece of penmanship he executed after making the decision. It bears the date of October 1906 and has a much closer resemblance to a printed type than the 'hand' he finally adopted. When 1 was there the following year, he was taking his hobby seriously.

From the first I had been impressed by the firmness, clearness, and the neatness of Arnold Bennett's hand-writing, but one night after dinner, he showed me the manuscript of an article he had written and was posting to London, in which these qualities were emphasised. I was so struck by it, I said that with a little extra effort he could make the manuscript of his next novel, one which would be unique.

This led to a discussion on the merits of margins, spacing, and general lay-out. He immediately searched his bookshelves for books possessing good qualities of this kind, and with these before us, we set about experimenting on sheets of paper, trying varying widths of margins and line spaces.

Having determined what we considered the most satisfactory proportions for these, I set them out on a piece of paper, the same size as his writing pad, and then ruled them in strong inked lines; the idea being that it could be placed under the rather transparent paper on which he was accustomed to write, and show faintly through it, so as to serve as a guide in keeping the margins and writing spaces orderly and uniform. On several subsequent evenings we devoted some hours to the forming of capital letters which would be easy to do with a pen, and which would be in harmony with writing that was related in form to lower-case types.

He spent some time in practising these, in preparation for the manuscript of his novel *The Old Wives' Tale*, and bearing on this, here is a quotation from his *French Journal*, dated 29th of July 1907, in which he says 'Fred Marriott says that yesterday was the hottest day he ever remembered. It ought to have been. In the afternoon I practised several formal hands for my novel. Marriott is an expert in calligraphy and he watched over me'.

Again, in the same journal I find this passage, dated 10th August 1907: 'At last I think I have evolved a fairly sound formal 'hand,' based on good calligraphic traditions, for my novel. I wrote a letter in it yesterday and showed it to Marriott to criticize; he found no fault with it at all; indeed, he was very complimentary. He said that if I wrote a whole long work in it, maintaining the standard, it would be unique in the modern world. I had the idea of doing the page in double columns, but he dissuaded me.

Now that the thing is settled, I want to begin the novel at once - example of the craftsman in a man trying to get the better of the artist. I can see the book written, and even bound by Bagguley of Newcastle-under-Lyme; and how beautiful it will be. But the thought of the labour of it frightens me at moments terribly; and I wonder whether I shall have the guts to go through with it.'

He did go through with it; with that dogged determination he invariably brought to bear on everything to which he set his mind. In my view it was a memorable achievement, and a rare example of sustained effort.

The rapidity with which he wrote that great manuscript was amazing to me. He became so dexterous, that he could write the formal type-like hand nearly as rapidly as he did his ordinary writing.

Years afterwards it occurred to me that a photographic reproduction in facsimile of *The Old Wives' Tale* manuscript would make a very remarkable volume, and be a work unique in the history of publishing. Consequently I wrote him saying I had a suggestion I would like to discuss with him, and asked him to appoint a time which would be convenient. He replied immediately, fixing the following afternoon, and I went and explained the scheme to which he listened with an imperturbable calm that rather damped my enthusiasm. Indeed, he showed very little interest, and it was evident that the idea didn't appeal to him. He thought it was impracticable; and he raised objections on the score of cost of production, on the insufficiency of people who would be interested enough to buy it, and moreover, that in any case the price of such a book would be prohibitive and doomed to failure.

I explained that I had never thought of it as a small priced publication, but rather as a book for collectors, and printed on fine paper, beautifully bound, and issued in a strictly limited edition of about seventy five or a hundred copies, at five or even ten guineas each. But I failed to convince him that it was a sound proposition.

However, I persistently referred to the subject on subsequent occasions, with the result that it was eventually produced, and was published by Messrs. Benn Bros. in an Edition de Luxe at five guineas.

I have seen the manuscript of the unfinished novel on which he was engaged when he was overtaken by his fatal illness. It displayed the same care and devotion to artistic appearances that characterised his manuscript of *The Old Wives' Tale;* so legible, orderly and finely spaced. It was as easy to read as a clear type.

Surely there has been no other author in modern times who has taken such pains to make book manuscripts so gratifying to handle and look upon.

38. WRITING RIGHT

As Marriott explains, it was Bennett's brother-in-law William Kennerley who, in the summer of 1906, identified calligraphy as a suitable hobby for the restless Bennett. A year later and Bennett felt able to confide in his *Journal* that he had mastered the art of calligraphy executed at speed. According to Kurt Koenigsberger, Kennerley had himself been studying Edward Johnston's 1906 influential *Writing & Illuminating & Lettering*, which 'emphasized calligraphy as more beautiful than - and indeed, the crucial influence upon - printing, and advocated "the transcribing and preservation of much good literature in this beautiful form"'.[136]

Working on the two volume *The Arnold Bennett Collection* catalogue of items held in the local history collection at the Potteries Museum & Art Gallery I was fascinated to find two examples of Bennett's calligraphy that provided the testing ground for his *The Old Wives' Tale* manuscript. One was a letter to his mother, in which his tells her that not only is it a personal letter but also a practice piece for later more extended effort: 'This is just an experiment I am making as to the form and look of a page in double column that I mean to adopt for a future manuscript that I have in mind. So I thought that I might as well kill two birds with one stone, and use the stuff for a letter to you'.[137] The other was a letter to his sister Tertia, confirming Marriot's involvement: 'I showed Frederick some specimens of the "hobby" which William decided I should take up, last summer in Normandy. He was much impressed, and said I should be able to do that sort of thing as well as anyone. He understands the principles of the thing as well as anyone... [and] is very clear and illuminating when he explains principles'.[138]

We have Marriott's aesthetic principles to thank for ensuring Bennett's continuing commitment to producing hand-written manuscripts and for persuading him to abandon the notion of double columns:

At last I think I have got into a fairly 'formed' formal hand for fine writing, and for the writing of my next novel [*The Old Wives' Tale}* in particular. I wrote a letter in it yesterday and gave it to Marriott to criticize. He found no fault with it at all. Indeed he was very enthusiastic about it and sent his wife up to look at it. ... Also that if I wrote a whole book keeping up to the standard, it would be unique in the world. When I lamented that one could not get a really black ink that would run through a fountain-pen, he said he preferred the slightly greyish tint of common ink. He dissuaded me from doing the novel in double columns.[139]

When Bennett posted the hand-written manuscript to his agent Pinker he called it 'an example of what MS. ought to be', and was at pains to insist that in having it typewritten in duplicate, 'the greatest possible care must be taken in handling the MS., which is extremely precious'.[140] Koenigsberger believes that such a curious announcement - that Bennett had produced 'what a manuscript ought to be' - puts us on notice that engaging the 'bibliographic coding network' and the material conditions surrounding it significantly occupied Bennett in the period of *The Old Wives' Tale*'s composition. Indeed, the form of the manuscript - as a calligraphically produced, illuminated manuscript - provoked a deal of worry in his *Journal:* 'I fear I should have to abandon this page and this handwriting for something larger and more cursive. And this I should regret'. For Bennett, the personal stakes were high for this *'precious'* piece of writing and by 1927 the success of the print version of the novel over two decades led the Ernest Benn firm to produce a limited edition of 500 signed copies of a full-colour photolithographic facsimile version of the manuscript of *The Old Wives' Tale.* It is an edition that flatters the eye and hand, even if there are few linguistic differences between the printed text and the manuscript text.

When considering the importance of the 1927 facsimile edition it is perhaps worth comparing it with the work of early twentieth-century modernists. However radical Ezra Pound's manifesto statements may have sounded, his early poems were modelled on medieval Tuscan and Provençal verse, and when he published his first collection of *The Cantos* they were ornately decorated in illuminated capitals and two-colour printing suggestive of Pre-Raphaelite design and bearing a striking resemblance to Bennett's *The Old Wives' Tale* manuscript title pages and chapter headings. In 1908, then, Pound and Bennett were united in acknowledging a debt to the Arts and Craft spirit of William Morris, demanding that printing and bookmaking should be an ideal synthesis of text, design and material culture.

Bennett's 'Author's Note' to the facsimile edition makes light of both his speed of calligraphic composition and of his artistic design:

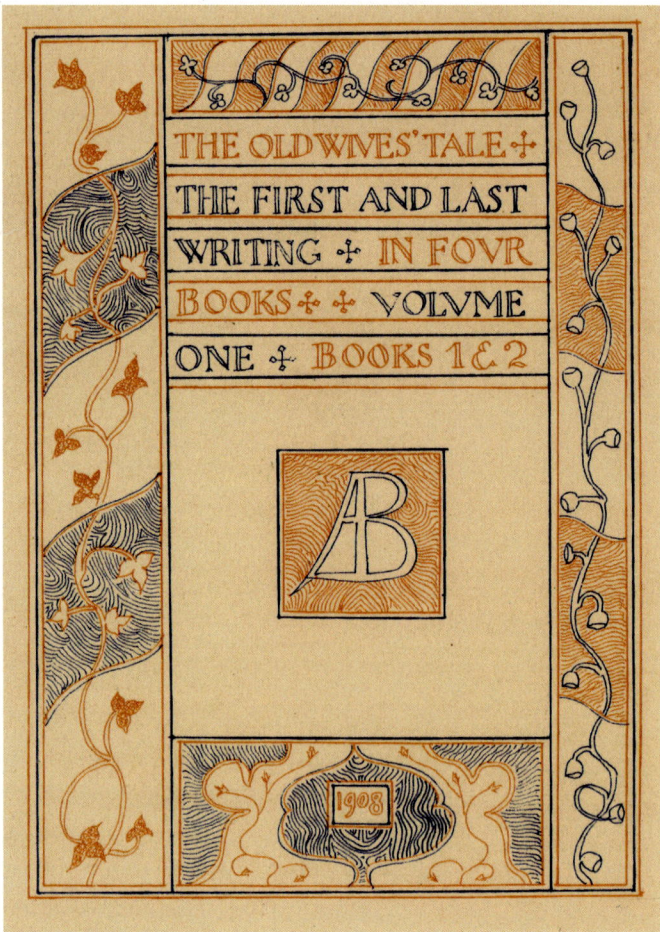

Bennett's illuminated manuscript for *The Old Wives' Tale*

Of course if your manuscript is to have even the most modest pretensions to calligraphic decency, you must know all the time exactly what you are about to do; otherwise a regular mess will ensue ... The reader, however, sees the worst of these messes; no page, so far as I remember, was destroyed and rewritten.

I offer no excuse for the title-pages. After doing a rough sketch for them in chalk, I drew them straight on the pages in two inks, designing as I went along: a case of sink or swim, do or die.[141]

For a more comprehensive history of his 'hobby' we can consult Bennett's revised *Journal* entries for the January1929 issue of Desmond MacCarthy's monthly *Life and Letters.* Here he gives details about his study of 'ancient models' and William Morris manuscripts. He details for the first time in MacCarthy's magazine the nuts and bolts of writing, the value of writing as a material practice beyond its rhetorical complexities:

> I had obtained the necessary apparatus of sloping boards, special paper, special pens, coloured inks. I soon saw that the chief thing, at any rate with my rather summary methods, was not the calligraphy but the general lay-out of the page-margins, etc. Walter Scott and Charlotte Brontë wrote lovely hands, but evidently the importance of the lay-out of the page never occurred to them. I have an idea that I can produce the most beautiful original manuscript of a novel that a novelist ever did produce. It will be the manuscript of *The Old Wives' Tale*.[142]

As can be deduced from Marriott's observation on the calligraphic beauty of Bennett's last unfinished novel, *Dream of Destiny*, I conclude that this 1927 'Note' to *The Old Wives' Tale* represents Bennett's devotion to manuscript and bibliographic practices from 1906 until his death. In his 1909 novel *The Glimpse*, Bennett appears as the thinly disguised central character who admits to books being one of the overwhelming passions of his life. In Chapter 23, 'The Palace', he goes into an extended two-page rapture over precisely the type of issues and values that underlie Bennett's *The Old Wives' Tale* manuscript production:

> I was a bookman; I had always been a bookman. From adolescence books had been one of my passions. Books not merely - and perhaps not chiefly - as vehicles of learning or knowledge, but books as books, books as entities, books as beautiful things, books as historical antiquities, books as repositories of memorable associations. Questions of type, ink, paper, margins, watermarks, paginations, bindings, were capable of really agitating me ... Radiant, light-giving, immaculate! To touch it was to thrill.[143]

The modern scholar, in his more liberated moments of emotional response, might well emulate Marriott's enthusiasm and enthuse over Bennett's illuminated manuscript. The 1927 facsimile - and here I might add that I own a signed copy of a limited edition of 500 -- is indeed the iconic representation of literary genius, the object beautiful that, with careful storage at the correct temperature in library archives, will keep its looks far longer than the Burslem of Bennett's youth it so memorably depicts.

39. BENNETT'S METHODS OF WORK

While the large circle of friends recognised that Arnold Bennett was a man endowed with glittering gifts, and felt that in the long run he would go far in his profession by the sheer force of his indomitable will, none could forecast the literary eminence to which he ultimately attained. Indeed, the first edition copies of his early books, which he generously presented to his relatives and particular friends, were subjected to very frank criticism by most of them. However, he never seemed to be unduly disturbed by these criticisms, and laughed at such as were merely dictated by what he termed the nonconformist conscience.

He resolutely set himself the task of conquering in the world of letters, and he succeeded to a greater degree than even he, with all his faith in his natural capacity could have imagined in the early days of our association.

It was interesting to observe how Arnold Bennett devoted his time, and how strictly he followed the plan he had laid down for himself. The driving force and vitality of his brain was always abundant, and he steadfastly pursued a straight line for the goal he had planned.

His work was of the utmost importance in his thoughts, and he wouldn't allow anything to interfere with it. His vivid and striking personality was manifest in all his work.

He had a clear conception of the value of his work to publishers, and he always asked, and insisted on getting, a good price for it; not with a set purpose of making money, but from a firm conviction of the justice of his demands.

The time of each day was apportioned to his various activities, in a kind of mental chart, to which, (save for an occasional days cycling recreation,) he rigidly adhered.

He rose regularly at 6.30 a.m., and after a light French breakfast consisting of buttered roll and coffee, he went for a walk into the forest to think out the subject matter for his days writing, which he confined to the mornings. In order to lessen the risk of distractions, he took the same route each morning. We were made aware of the extent and direction of his perambulations, and we were careful to avoid interference with its seclusion when we took our morning walks.

On his return, he went straight to his study and settled down to his writing for three hours, and it was understood that he was not to be disturbed. He wrote very rapidly, and his manuscripts were extraordinarily free from erasions and alterations. I believe in this he was rather exceptional.

His writing, for the day, was finished by noon, and then he devoted half an hour to piano practise before lunch. Lunch over; a general state of somnolence prevailed for about three quarters of an hour, which was an indulgence in the cause of health; and was taken on the advice of his doctor.

If the weather was kind, we went out together with our sketching stools and painting materials, and sketched for the remainder of the afternoon. On wet afternoons, Bennett would either practise drawing, or paint a still-life subject in water-colour, consisting of bric-a-brac and flowers, or of a portion of the interior of one of the rooms.

Dinner was characteristically French, and was taken leisurely; usually occupying an hour, during which all sorts of topics were discussed.

Though Bennett at that time seldom took wine himself it was always there for others. I particularly remember an excellent red wine he had, and when I remarked upon its fine quality, he asked if I could guess what it cost? I confessed that I couldn't, but I said I could tell him approximately what he would have to pay for it in London restaurants, and I quoted five or six shillings a bottle. He laughed, and said, 'Well it is the best wine I could get in Bordeaux when I was staying there. I ordered a large cask of it and had it bottled here in Fontainebleau, and it cost exactly 5d a bottle'.

It was an illuminating revelation of the amount of money absorbed in customs duties and retailer's profits on wine.

Sometimes after dinner, we had music in the manner of our Chelsea days; and Arnold would coach me in some of his favourite Schubert songs, or practise a bit of Beethoven. Or if we felt we required exercise, we all walked in the forest, and Mrs. Bennett would collect varieties of 'Champignon' which were abundant. She was expert in knowledge of the kinds that were edible, and moreover, knew how best to cook them. As some of them looked like the brilliantly coloured fungoid growths prevalent in our English woods, we were rather nervous about eating them, but as no gastric complications followed after our first venture, we ate them after without misgivings.

40. ALL IN A DAY

Marriott's contribution to the legend of Bennett as a punctilious writer whose every day is first and foremost devoted to his craft with a 'straight line for the goal he had planned' in mind, is somewhat at odds with the rather more playful character, ever ready to wander off in Parisian labyrinths, that we encounter in his 13 December, 1903 *Journal* entry:

After buying papers and tea yesterday I lunched at the little creamery in the Place de la Trinité. Then I came home and read various papers and periodicals and 'Casanova', and fell asleep, sleeping uncomfortably. Then I tried seriously to find the ideas for chapter 11 of [*A Great Man*]; I had been more or less asking for them all morning; no success. Then I went out for a walk, and felt tired even in starting. I walked through the St. Lazare quarter to the Madeleine and turned along the Grand Boulevard to the Grand Café. I like the interior of this café It is much more like the respectable ugliness of an English club as anything in Paris. I ordered a cup of chocolate because I felt empty.

I thought steadily for one hour over this chocolate. And I seemed to leave the café with one or two germs of ideas. I walked home, cogitating. When I arrived, there was a telegram... requiring my weekly article two days earlier than usual. This upset my plans somewhat. I felt so tired - I had taken a chill - that I lay down on the eiderdown on the bed and went to sleep again, reading 'Casanova'.

When I awoke it was dark. I made tea and felt better. A leading notion for the chapter had now formed itself. I went to the Comédie Mondaine to book a seat for Brieux's 'Berceau', and then to the Duval to dine, where I read *Le Temps* all through. Then I bought a cigar and had a coffee in the Place Clichy. I cogitated at the café for an hour, and then I had the whole chapter clearly outlined in my head. This is a fair specimen of one of my cogitating days.[144]

Here, in a journal entry that successfully mimics Bennett's admiration for the Goncourt brother's journal, we have a portrait of the artist as a laid-back *flâneur* that I for one find it easy to warm to.

In addition to presenting first editions of his books to friends and relatives, Bennett also dedicated ten of them to important people in his life, some of whom would be little known today were it not for the Bennett connection.[145] Bennett's first novel, *A Man from the North,* is unique in not naming its dedicatee, although it is easy for us to guess the identity of 'To the one to whom I most honour' as belonging to his mother, Sarah Ann. Seen as unassertive but strong willed she provided the emotional stability for a family of nine children. 'She was to appear from time to time in her son's journal, usually stepping forth from the shadow of illness or death. "I don't like that woman at all," she grumbled after seeing Carmen at Hanley, and her sons and daughters cherished the remark and quoted it with laughing remembrance long after.' [146]

Bennett's 1904 novel *A Great Man: A Frolic* is dedicated to Marriott: 'To my dear friend Frederick Marriott and to the imperishable memory of old times'. Given what we know from Marriott's memoir of his love of fun and frolics, including picking friends' pockets, the novel's sub-title appears particularly apposite. Highly praised at the time by friends, the novel today is critically neglected. This is unfortunate because the story, far from being a mere frolic, undertakes an astute deconstruction of certain commercial, as opposed to aesthetic, aspects of Edwardian publishing practices, in which:

... worthless trash succeeds because rapaciously fabricated sales figures are bolstered by aggressive advertising. The public demands value for money, and valorises narrative length over artistic merit. Celebrity status is confirmed honorifically, irrespective of artistic talent. Literary agents are the only prophylactics against the extortions of unprincipled and parochially incompetent publishers who fail to recognise the lucrative potential of the burgeoning American market. Press reviews are venal and commercially self-serving. The professional theatre is at the mercy of entrepreneurial poseurs, fraudsters and egocentrics.[147]

The dedication that really intrigued me, however, sending me off along another labyrinthine literary pathway, was that to Roy Devereux in *Whom God Hath Joined* (1906). Mrs. Roy Devereux (Margaret Rose Roy Pemberton-Devereux) wrote for Bennett when he was editor of *Woman*, and on the evidence of Bennett's *Journals*, continued a very close friendship with him in Paris, even to the extent of involving herself in the ill-fated introduction to Eleanor Green. James Hepburn reproduces an intimate conversation with her on 2 July 1904 that is absent from the published *Journals*:

She could talk of nothing but her heart, & I wanted to talk of nothing better. I said it was singular I had never got up a passion for her, & she said she supposed it was singular: 'Because in some ways', I suppose,' she said, 'I must be the most attractive woman you have ever known in your life.' To that I sincerely agreed. When she had told me all about her affairs (I don't know why I should tell you all these things, she said), I told her all about mine, & pretty considerably astonished her. She said she thought I had done very well for myself.[148]

Two days later finds Bennett still contemplating the pleasure taken in her company, and we can glean his sense of freedom at being able to talk intimately with a woman about sexual matters in a manner more appropriate to the all-male London club scene:

> The other evening Mrs. D. had said some man had said to her that for a first-class man there could be nothing between a *cocotte* and a *grande dame*; it must be either the one or the other. ... I should say it is very true. The only question is whether, for a man ferociously egoist, the advantages and disadvantages of the *cocotte* and of the *grande dame* respectively are not about the equal. I think they are. I know that when we were dining last night at Marguéry's and talking purely personal gossip, I had a feeling of contentment which I should like to have a bit oftener.[149]

But other than appearances in Bennett's *Journals*, the clearly liberated Mrs. Roy then virtually disappears from critical literary discourse, despite penning several well-received novels and volumes of journalism. One of the latter, *Side Lights on South Africa*, Bennett reviewed in *Hearth and Home* magazine (28 December, 1899) praising its author as 'one of the most talented women journalists in London' with 'an exceptionally good style'. It is only now, in the twenty-first century, that Devereux's work is receiving close attention in the wake of the rediscovery of the fiction of the New Woman prompted by the second-wave women's movement in the 1970s.

For all her liberated attitude to life, including cultivating the company of interesting men, Devereux had a conflicted relationship with the rise of the New Woman, in much the same way as did her contemporary, Sarah Grand. Expressing her views on 'The Feminine Potential' in the *Saturday Review* (22 June, 1895) she regrets that 'life has taken on a strange unloveliness, and the least beautiful thing therein is the New *Woman*'. As Ann Heilmann eloquently put it in her *The Late-Woman Question; A Collection of Key Texts*, Devereux 'tried to combine the intellectual New Woman with the "archaizing, mystical, sensual Pre-Raphaelite type"'.[150]

This description marries with another recent study rehabilitating feminist writers of the 1890s by Talia Schaffer: '[Devereux combined] fashion-magazine scolding and Ruskin exaltation. Devereux's *The Ascent of Woman* (1896) is an aesthetic fashion manual designed for the New Woman'.[151] Devereux surely deserves a place in the scholarly revision of first-wave literary feminism; a project requiring access to original sources, unfortunately not readily available in her case. And this is where Bennett's prolific but uncollected 1890s journalism has such an important part to play. Neither Heilmann nor Schaffer are aware that the one Devereux book title they both single out for critical attention is the lead review in Bennett's *Woman* 'Book Chat' column of 3 June, 1896. Reprinted here for the first time it represents, along with 'The Brontë Relics at Haworth', just a fraction of the treasure house of Bennett 'Book Chat' articles awaiting inclusion in the literary revisionism of key 1890s texts:

●●●●●●●●●●●●●●●●●

The Ascent of Woman

'In a toilette,' says Mrs. Roy Devereux, the author of *The Ascent of Woman* (John Lane, 3s 6d. net), 'as in a piece of painting or of prose, the presence or absence of style determines the value of the work, and if this one thing needful should be lacking, no other excellence will suffice to bring it within the province of art'. Well and simply said! And because I find myself in hearty concord with the proposition, it falls to me to say that the omnipresence of a distinguished style determines for me the value of this book. There are those who will admire it for its subtle and sagacious diagnosis of the case of the modern woman; or for the 'most clear vision' of a future ideal, so delicately adumbrated in the introduction, and in Chapter VI of Part 1; or for the spacious, authentic culture which informs every page; or for its fine moderation, or its aloofness from the obvious, or its wit, or its courage. But as for me, though I am blind to none of these excellences, I take my chief delight in the mere style. I cannot but think that Mrs Devereux has formed her habit of writing upon that of Renan. She has all his grace, and much of his delicious, limpid clarity, and if at times she is too munificent in metaphor we must remember that this is her first book and attribute the indiscretion to the excusable full-handedness of youth ..... or perhaps this prodigality, like the author's use of a plural verb after 'none' is intentional, and designed to serve the function of the beauty-spot of yore. Be that as it may, there can be no kind of doubt that we have here a prose style which, for distinction, for elaborate finish, and for music, can stand against that of any Englishwoman living or dead.

The book is divided into two sections - 'Of Her Life,' and 'Of Her Looks,' and it is the first of these which seriously counts; the second I regard as dessert - something 'nice but unnecessary' to the elucidation of Mrs. Devereux's message. What that message is I cannot well define, at any rate in the space at my disposal. For throughout the book one is conscious of a certain high reticence on the part of the author. She will not tell you all her thoughts about the possibilities of the feminine; she does not wear her heart on her ballon sleeve, nor is she capable of 'sprinkling her person with every trinket she owns.' One fact shines clear, namely, that while eager for progress and the casting-off of fetters, she is singularly free from the worst of all prejudices - the prejudice of the reformer. Her temper is fastidiously eclectic, and everything which makes for unloveliness and the loss of dignity comes under her silken lash. Also, it is made evident, rather by implication than explicitly, that she entertains a mighty disregard for what 'other people' think. No opposing and vituperative majority, whether of Belgravia or Brixton will ruffle her serenity. She will not even pay to the unreflecting crowd the compliment of condemning its stolid inertia; she chooses to ignore it. And yet her views, far from being 'wild' or 'visionary' or anything of that sort, are studiously and sanely moderate. She is the advertiser of no patent nostrum for the cure of that particular 'malady of the century' which is her theme. Time and faith and patience are her medicines, and therein lies her title to respect.

On page 18 I observe a passage which happily discloses both the intention of Mrs. Devereux's book and the philosophic spirit which animates it. I will quote, and have done: - 'She [the woman that is called "new"] is regarded not as an evolution inevitable as any other process, but as an excrescence on the face of Society, the fungus-like growth of a night. Because the environment out of which she has arisen, and the spiritual conditions of which she is the expression, are not obvious to the superficial critic, the new woman is today the jest of every fool and the bugbear of every philosopher. Her enemies will have none of her; her partisans find no fault in her at all. But neither of them has ever swept the mind clear of prejudice and sat down to analyse her essential elements. And yet to gauge the extension of her life is to appreciate its significance and to understand her aspirations is to honour them in a 'measure'. To gauge, to appreciate, to understand: that is Mrs. Devereux's honourable aim, and, in compassing it, she has contrived to give us the most brilliant analysis of typical modern femininity, its strengths and its weaknesses, which I have been fortunate enough to meet with.[152]

● ● ● ● ● ● ● ● ● ● ● ● ● ● ● ● ●

Having dedicated *The Old Wives' Tale* in 1908 to William Kennerley, who married Bennett's sister Tertia, there are to be no more dedications for 22 years until that for George Reeves-Smith, a director of the Savoy Hotel, in *Imperial Palace* (1929), Bennett's last completed published novel.

The Potteries Museum & Art Gallery houses a major collection of Bennett's many watercolours and drawings, including several done in Marriott's company in France. The one shown here, of Villa des Néfliers, must have been painted on one of those days when 'the weather was kind'. The most detailed account to date of Bennett as an artist is to be found in Catherine Goodwin's 'Bennett and Art' illustrated essay in *An Arnold Bennett Companion*. She judiciously observes that his 'watercolours vary in quality from some accomplished works, including some well executed landscapes of Holland and France, to others of inferior quality'.[153] Painting was a hobby, meant to be relaxing, but even so, Bennett constantly sought expert guidance on improving his technique, and could become very frustrated when his efforts fell short of the professional standards he had set himself.

Villa de Néfliers, watercolour and pencil on board

41. GLASGOW

I can remember being very much astonished in the early days of Arnold Bennett's activities as a playwright, at the number of plays he sold to actor managers or theatrical proprietors and which were never produced! Several of his plays were taken on payment of a hundred pounds or so, under an agreement that if they were not performed within a specified time they should be returned to the author. Knowing the comparatively short time he took in writing them, I thought at the time the terms were generous, and came to the conclusion that if his was the common experience of playwrights, there were large sums of money expended on unproduced plays.

Some time after he had completed writing *The Great Adventure* he called at my studio and told me that it was going to be produced at the Glasgow Repertory Theatre, and that he was going up there to attend the rehearsals, and see the first night performance. I said, 'By Jingo Arnold, I'd like to go with you', and it was immediately arranged that we should make the journey together.

I was much more excited over the affair than he was, and on the day for our departure I was at Euston station some time before the train was timed to leave, and spent some uneasy minutes wondering whether he would arrive in time. But although he ran it very close, he had time to find the compartment in which he had previously reserved two corner seats.

On arrival at Glasgow, we were met by Alfred Wareing the Manager of the Repertory Theatre, and I made the pleasant discovery that we were old friends, for he had studied under my direction at the Goldsmiths' Institute School of Art, in his early youth.

After we had dined at the hotel, we went along to Wareing's house and there met the producer and the leading members of the company who were engaged for the play. We all sat round the fire discussing theatrical matters in general, but the talk centred particularly round the production of *The Great Adventure*.

It was interesting to learn how it was that the play came to be first produced in Glasgow. It transpired that while Wareing was passing through Paris on his way back from Corsica, he accepted an invitation from Bennett to spend an evening with him at his flat, and it was an inevitable result of a meeting between a theatre manager and a playwright that the conversation should turn to the subject of plays.

The Great Adventure had recently been returned by a famous actor-manager, and as Bennett was certain that if given a trial it would prove successful, he freely expressed his opinions of theatre managers. They were uncomplimentary.

Wareing asked if he might see the play, and it was agreed that he should take it away and read it during the remainder of his journey. He was so impressed by it, that on arrival in London he telegraphed to his co-directors in Glasgow his intention to produce it at the opening of the next season. Indeed, he had so much faith in it that he was anxious to secure the world rights of it, but while his proposal was still under discussion, the rights were secured by Granville Barker.

The conversation was interspersed with amusing anecdotes of theatrical life within the experience of the members of the profession present, with an occasional more highly flavoured funny story thrown in as opportunity occurred. It was close on midnight when we dispersed.

Next morning we were at the theatre by ten o'clock to watch the progress of a rehearsal.

●●●●●●●●●●●●●●●●●

RESTORED TEXT

I had some previous experience of theatrical rehearsals, For while I was employed as designer for Messrs Marcus Ward & Co., in the early eighties, I was engaged to design the programme covers for some of the Gilbert & Sullivan operas and I had to attend rehearsals to make drawings of some of the principal characters. Thus I became a privileged witness of some of W. S. Gilbert's spirited criticisms and exacting instructions, to those engaged in the early productions of some of the most successful series of Light Operas of this generation.

I also attended rehearsals of the successful musical comedy 'Dorothy' in which Miss Marie Tempest, Ben Davie sand Haydn Griffiths played the principal roles, and for which I designed the programme.

●●●●●●●●●●●●●●●●

I was very much impressed by the skill and unflagging energy which Frank Vernon the producer brought to bear on the rehearsals of *The Great Adventure*. His close attention to subtle detail and to general effect was amazing. Indeed, there were so many suggestions, criticisms and alterations, and the prompter was in such frequent requisition, that I couldn't imagine how the play could possibly be got ready in time for the opening night.

From his observation post in the stalls, Bennett made occasional suggestions to the producer as to the effects he wanted, which were immediately acted upon with good results.

As I sat there watching all the work in progress, I came to the conclusion that the theatrical profession must be the most nerve-racking of all the professions, and I certainly felt no desire to enter the ranks of either actors or producers.

Bennett was besieged by press-men seeking interviews, and by camera-men who wanted to photograph him. As we walked together in the streets in company with Alfred Wareing, photographers would suddenly appear, and 'snap' us in the act, and the results of their efforts appeared in the daily papers. Finished proofs of these photographs were left at our Hotel for our 'kind acceptance'.

I have a vivid recollection of the thrills I felt as a witness of the first really big press boom accorded to Arnold Bennett, which he accepted in the most matter-of-fact manner, as if he had been used to it all his life, and was his common experience,

It was at such times that he exercised an inflexible determination to cover with an impenetrable disguise, any signs of the emotion he might be inwardly feeling.

When we got to the theatre for the opening performance and were talking to the members of the cast, I was surprised to find them all confessing to feeling very nervous; for they had given no indication of suffering from nerves during the progress of the rehearsals.

The theatre was crowded to capacity, and the play had a very enthusiastic reception throughout, and when the curtain was lowered at the conclusion of the last act, the applause was loud and spontaneous from every part of the house.

As it was known that Bennett was in the theatre there were repeated calls of 'Author! Author! Speech, Speech!', but he couldn't be prevailed upon to respond. He was far too shy for that kind of publicity, and immediately retired into the far corner of the box we occupied, well out of sight.

As soon as the theatre began to clear, we made our way to the back of the stage where there followed a general interchange of unstinted congratulations between author, manager, producer, and performers, on the brilliant success of the play, while grease paint and other multifarious make-up was in process of removal.

It was a very jovial company that gathered afterwards at Wareing's house, and remained talking over the adventures of the first-night production of *The Great Adventure* until the small hours of the morning.

• • • • • • • • • • • • • • • • •

RESTORED TEXT

While we were up there, we took the opportunity of visiting the Glasgow School of Art, which had the reputation of being one of the best in the Kingdom. The headmaster, Mr. Francis Newbury, was well known to me for he had been a fellow student at South Kensington, and I was acquainted with all the instructors in the school save one; the instructor of modelling.

The school occupied an imposing granite structure designed by Charles R. Mackintosh, an architect with a wide vision well in advance of his time, and Bennett was always attracted by any new forms of artistic expression, was at once impressed by the arresting austerity of the exterior, which relied entirely upon the structural requirements for its decorative features. No carved enrichments in the way of mouldings round the window openings or cornice, which I believe was without precedent in those days. Surely this, and other buildings by this architect must have exercised a considerable influence upon the modern movements in architecture, both in Britain and on the Continent, and anticipated much of the simplified style of building prevalent today.

At that time the Glasgow School of Art was reputed to be the best equipped of any in the Kingdom, but it is questionable whether it still holds that proud position, because the London County Council and similar bodies up and down the country have since lavished large sums of money on Art School equipment.

We were shown one piece of equipment which was quite new to us, consisting of an electrically heated 'throne' in which the living models were posed. It was an ingenious device, which made it possible for the model to be kept warm, without making the rest of the studio uncomfortably over-heated for the rest of the students.

Most studios in which male models are posed have to be kept at temperatures round about 70 degrees, and even then some models will complain of feeling cold, while the students are in a continual state of perspiration.

Having regard for the reputation the Scotch people have for clannishness, it struck Arnold Bennett as remarkable that there was no Scotch professors on the teaching staff! Maurice Greiffenhagen R.A. was professor of Painting, Professor R. Anning Bell R.A. taught the classes in decorative painting and Book Illustration, Arthur Nicholas taught design, and the modelling classes were taught by either a Belgian or Dutchman!

● ● ● ● ● ● ● ● ● ● ● ● ● ● ● ● ●

The members of the Glasgow Artists' Society gave a dinner at their Club in honour of Bennett, which was attended by a number of eminent writers, artists, and art collectors.

Mr. J.R. Richmond a wealthy art collector, was present at the dinner, and next day he took us to his house to see his collection of pictures, which comprised many notable and valuable works, including a number of fine examples of the French Romanticists.

Richmond was a partner in the great engineering firm of Messrs G. and J, Weir & Co., the most famous steam pump manufacturers in the world, and he took us over their immense factory, which was a model of orderly organisation that profoundly impressed Bennett. Moreover, he very kindly put his motor car and chauffeur at our disposal, and so enabled us to tour the fine stretches of country round Glasgow.

Wareing introduced us to Neil Munro the novelist, a man of great charm, whose work both as journalist and novelist Bennett greatly admired. A new novel by Munro had just been published by Blackwood, entitled 'The New Road', which many reviewers considered was his greatest work. He joined us in our car-runs to Loch Lomond and other popular show places, and to the then busy ship-building yards.

It was very interesting to listen to the views exchanged between Bennett and Munro about their methods of work, places, people, and general debatable topics.

42. ON STAGE

Marriott's surprise that whilst several of Bennett's early plays were commissioned and purchased by actor managers or theatre owners, they never took up the option to produce them, directs us towards a little known aspect of Bennett's early writing career. He wrote some 16 plays - only one of which, *Rivals for Rosamund,* was ever produced in his life-time - before finding commercial success in 1908 with *Cupid and Commonsense,* adapted from his novel *Anna of the Five Towns.* Then, from 1908 to 1913 he had four further plays running on the London stage, and by 1913 there had been some 2,700 performances of his plays around the world, helping make Bennett a wealthy man. Nevertheless, payment for his early unproduced scripts provided a welcome addition to Bennett's income at a time when his future financial security was far from guaranteed. They now await proper critical scrutiny if we are to have a comprehensive analysis of Bennett's early working methods, together with a critical insight into his ready willingness to collaborate successfully with fellow writers.

In 2005 I was invited by Catherine Goodwin, Collections Officer, at the Potteries Museum & Art Gallery, to help with cataloguing their extensive Bennett collection, encompassing paintings, drawings, photographs, books, personal objects, letters, and , most importantly in the context of the above, unpublished hand-written and/or typed play manuscripts.[154] The Museum's Bennett Collection was found to house eight of these original manuscripts, including collaborative efforts with Eden Phillpotts, Fred Alcock, Henry Davray, and Arthur Hooley. An important aspect of their value lies in allowing us to observe close up the creative workings of a writer's mind as corrections and amendments to first drafts create dense architectural textual palimpsests conducive to scholarly exegesis; for *The Duke's Sacrifice* (1902-3)Bennett even included a drawing of his design for the stage-set.

Not that Bennett the early dramatist had anything other than strictly financial interests in mind, as his February 1901 letter to his friend George Sturt makes very clear:

I have cleared off all plays for the present. The Hooley-Bennett partnership has proved extraordinarily successful. I hoped much from it, but it has surprised me .Considering we raked in £275 solid cash in the first year, getting two plays accepted, I reckon we can please ourselves, for the theatrical ring is a very difficult one to enter, far more so than the purely literary.... When Maude [lessee of the Haymarket Theatre] asked us for a 1 act play we each wrote one (in 3 Days), & it was mine that was took. We think little of that piece however; it is the big play that is going to make the big splash. I need not tell you that, so far, we attach no artistic importance whatever to anything we have done, but we hope in the future to write an artistic farce. Money is our aim solely; Arthur wants to write poetry & me fiction.[155]

Bennett and Hooley collaborated in 1900 on *The Chancellor* and *The Wayward Duchess*; it was Bennett's *The Post Mistress* 'that was took'. Whilst they were fatalistic about the chances of the 'big play', *The Wayward Duchess*, being produced they nevertheless had the confidence of youth in their joint efforts: 'Arthur Hooley & I have finished the first act (& the outline of the rest) of the four act romantic drama which we are doing for Cyril Maude.... the thing (on its plane) is damn good. Arthur Hooley says it is bloody good - extra bloody; & he may be right.'[156]

Bennett's enjoyment of his time in Glasgow, and in particular his meeting with a future friend-to-be, John Richmond, is clearly apparent in a letter home to Marguerite:

I must say I am very well treated on my travels. Neil Munro, Scotland's foremost novelist, was waiting at the station yesterday evening with Richmond. It was a courtesy. We dined together with Richmond at the Conservative Club. Then we went to Richmond's to chat and smoke.... I have the most awesome day today, in factories etc., followed by a party at the Arts club. Richmond is sending his car for me at 10.30. The greatest advantage of being a novelist whose novels are liked by serious people is that one is treated better than a prince. [157]

Richmond was later invited to visit Comarques, where he took the opportunity to observe Arnold and Marguerite's relationship close-up; 'He had himself always well under control. I have seen Marguerite irritate him beyond measure yet he always retained control of himself and remained calm outwardly and uniformly courteous'. Outward calm could be deceptive - Bennett avoided confrontations by communicating with his wife by passing her a series of notes even when they were both within the same four walls. Such 'courtesy' came at significant emotional cost to both parties.

Bennett and Marriott in Glasgow.

43. SIMON FUGE

After one of Arnold Bennett's lengthy periods on the Continent, he paid us a surprise visit one morning, and when our conversation had spread to general topics after an introductory exchange of news, he remarked on several structural alterations we had made, and changes we had effected in the arrangement of furniture, pictures and bric-a-brac. During lunch he told us that one of the objects of his visit was to refresh his memory with details of the house and surroundings as a background for a novel he was going to write. It transpired that it was for his novel entitled *Simon Fuge*.

His remarkable powers of observation and the facility with which he recorded his impressions always amazed me. He made very few notes in writing, but I knew that he had absorbed all the material he required for the work he had in hand. There is abundant evidence of his trained faculties of observation and memory in his novels, notably in such books as *The Old Wives' Tale* and *The Imperial Palace* [sic], the latter being an astonishingly minute record of the complicated problems continually confronting the managers of such huge undertakings.

Although I have been a smoker for over fifty years, he more than once declared that I didn't know how to smoke. I believe it hurt him to watch me smoke cigars, because he considered I always smoked them too quickly. A cigar to him was a thing to linger over and toy with.

Once after we had lunched together, in the early days of his affluence, he handed me his cigar case, saying, 'Here Frederick, have a Corona Corona'. When we had both finished them, I took out my modest case, and said, 'Here Arnold, have a Marcella Marcella'; with a merry twinkle in his eye he declined, saying, he didn't smoke boy's cigars.

Sometimes when we were smoking and I had perpetrated a particularly silly joke, he would lean forward with mock solemnity and say, 'Let me see Frederick, how old are you?' and then he would break out into one of his upper- register staccato laughs. A kindly but effective admonition which left no sting, because I knew that he enjoyed the frivolity.

44. A GOOD CIGAR

By general consent 'The Death of Simon Fuge', published in the collection *The Grim Smile of the Five Towns* (1907), is Bennett's outstanding contribution to the art and craft of short story writing. It is fitting that a fellow Potteries writer, John Wain, called it 'the most delicate product of Bennett's art'[158] with resonances of Chekhovian introspection. Bennett's February 1909 *Journal* entry shows him aiming for just such an endorsement, albeit with a somewhat uncharacteristic modest coda:

> More and more struck by Tchekoff, and more and more inclined to write a lot of very short stories in the same technique. As a fact, 'The death of Simon Fuge', written long before I had read Tchekoff, is in the same technique, and about as good. Though to say anything is as good as 'Ward No.6' in 'the Black Monk', wants a bit of nerve.[159]

In brief, Bennett narrates the story through the eyes of a cosmopolitan outsider, Loring, visiting The Potteries for the first time, having read of the death of the Bursley born artist Simon Fuge, whom he had known in London. At first shocked by the grime of an industrial landscape and suspicious of its inhabitants artistic taste, he is won round by his host, local architect Robert Brindley's, hospitality and obvious enjoyment of and participation in home-grown artistic endeavours. As for Fuge's hints of a sexual night-time dalliance on a local lake with two women, it turns out to have been a harmless lark.

I am intrigued by the thread that scrolls out across the years from local author Bennett to local author John Wain, a thread that makes Wain supremely qualified to understand and critique the work of a writer who had to distance himself from his provincial background in order to appreciate its universal merits as source material for his novels. Wain was born in, and spent the first 18 years of his life in The Potteries, regarding it as a stroke of good luck to have grown up in an industrial region, believing such environments to be difficult to penetrate and understand if one comes to them from outside. He, like Bennett, moved away - to Oxford and Paris - publishing his debut novel *The Contenders* in1958, a novel that relives exactly the urge to tear up domestic roots and be free that faced the young Bennett:

> If I can't name this town [Stoke], I'll just call it 'the town I mustn't name'. Anyway, it's that place you stop at on the way to Manchester - the one where you look out of the train window when it's slowing down, and think, 'Well, at least I don't live here'. We did live there, however; for that matter I still do, as I said, on the local paper. Yes, people actually do live in this place. All English towns fall into one

of two categories, those that people live in because they like them, and those that people live in while they make enough money to be able to leave and go and live in the other kind.

For the moment I'll just make the obvious point that the mere fact of being brought up in a town where everything was shabby, dirty, dwarfish, peeling and generally lousy as another thing that helped to make most of us competitive. You looked round you as you stood waiting for the bus to take you to school, and you thought, 'If I don't do well I might have to end up staying here.[160]

This is Wain as literary avatar; Bennett's sole *Journal* entry for 20 October, 1927 reads: 'I took the 12.5 back to London, which went through the Potteries. The sight of this district gave me a shudder.' [161]

The Industrial Potteries.

45. COMARQUES

After the success of his novel *The Old Wives' Tale* and of the play *Milestones*, which he wrote in collaboration with his friend Edward Knoblock, Arnold Bennett found himself in such affluent circumstances that he was able to possess a yacht, an ambition he had cherished for some years.

He bought a commodious Dutch yacht called the Velsa, which he kept at Brightlingsea in Essex. As a consequence of that, and of his friendship with John Atkins, who also possessed a yacht, and lived in Essex, he was desirous of living somewhere near that part of the coast, in order that he could carry on his work free from the social interruptions of London, and be in the vicinity of his yacht.

I remember his making several fruitless excursions in company with his friend Atkins in search of a house which would supply the modern equipment and standard of comfort he required. They viewed many houses, but for one reason or another, none of them fully answered his purpose.

In addition to the luxurious yacht, he had bought a Lanchester Car, which was then the best car on the market; so it was an easy matter for him to pursue his quest.

He liked an old house at Thorpe-le-Soken which had been built by French Huguenot refugees, but as it was devoid of modern conveniences he didn't think seriously about it.

However, when he took his wife (Marguerite) round the district to look at some other houses which were advertised for sale -- none of which found favour - she asked him to take her to see the old Huguenot house he had spoken of. When she saw it, she immediately fell in love with it, and saw the possibilities of both the house and its extensive grounds. Probably the Huguenot associations with the place had some influence on her enthusiastic appreciation of it.

Then followed consultations with Rickards the architect, who went down with Arnold and inspected the property with a view to estimating the probable cost of alterations and additions; new bathrooms, decorations, lighting etc., and eventually a letting contract was signed for four years, with the option of purchase at a fixed price, at the end of that time.

The house had the attractive name of 'Comarques', which, added to Thorpe-le-Soken, made a distinctive address.

A good sum of money was spent on alterations to the house and improvements to the gardens, as well as a tennis court on which I had many good games with Bennett who usually won, but I got some comfort from being able to clear the net at a standing jump, which he couldn't do. He played all over the court, combining drives from the base line, half volleys in the middle of the court and close volleys from the net, and though some of his strokes were very fast, they had calculated placing which kept me continually running about.

At the end of the four years he bought the property, and lived there until 1921, when he sold it and returned to London.

Many times I went down there for a day's sketching, and I used to catch the 5a.m. newspaper train from Liverpool Street station arriving at Thorpe-le-Soken in good time for breakfast, returning by the last train at night, which gave me a good long day.

I spent the mornings sketching in the immediate neighbourhood, but in the afternoons Bennett always joined me, bringing his sketching kit, and we went in his car to places farther afield, both inland and along the coast for variety of subject material. Occasionally our mutual friend Rickards joined us in these excursions, to the enlivenment of the proceedings.

Sometimes my wife, our little daughter Menetta and I were invited to spend a week at Comarques, where we had very delightful times, and thoroughly explored that part of Essex.

During one of our visits Menetta contracted mumps, and had to be left behind with her 'Uncle' Arnold, and 'Aunty' Marguerite, until the doctor had completed the cure. After a little scene she had created early one morning, Bennett recited the following limerick during breakfast:

> There was a young girl named Menetta
> Who was ill and wouldn't get better,
> She tried it is said, to crawl under the bed,
> And wept when her Aunt wouldn't let her.

At that time, and long afterwards, Menetta was under the impression that they were real relatives, and was very disappointed when she discovered that she was only a spurious niece.

It is very pleasant to recall the happy times we spent at Comarques with Arnold Bennett and his wife, sharing the amenities of life which success had brought, and which were lavishly extended to their friends at all times.

When I paid one of my surprise visits to Comarques in the early days of the great war, I found that troops were stationed at Thorpe-le-Soken taking part in the defences of the East coast, and the village had become very active.

Arnold Bennett and his wife were doing everything they could for the benefit of the troops. They had a large wooden hut constructed in their grounds, and equipped it with a stage and piano, tables, chairs, and a good variety of games, such as chess, draughts, cards etc. It constituted a kind of club house which was available for the recreation of the soldiers whenever they pleased.

There was a plentiful supply of tea, coffee, and soft drinks served by Mrs. Bennett and willing helpers from the village whom she enlisted to assist with the work.

Entertainments were organised which discovered talented performers among the officers and men of the army, and augmented by local talent. These entertainments provided a rich fund of pleasure for all concerned, and were much appreciated. Arnold Bennett was so busily engaged in London on official work, that he couldn't actively cooperate in these jolly affairs, which were entirely arranged by his wife. I well remember the pride with which she told me that she had sung an old French popular song at one of the concerts, and that 'the Tommies loved it'. With a characteristic ripple of laughter, she said, 'And now I am the favourite artiste of the company'.

As many officers as their house would accommodate were billeted with the Bennetts, and they made full use of the tennis courts in their leisure time. Bennett and I occasionally played against them with varying success.

Bennett did very useful propaganda work during the war, and he sent me a copy of a small book which he published at the end of 1914, entitled, *Liberty, a statement of the British case*, and on the fly-leaf he wrote the following: 'To F.M. from A.B. Written, by request, for the American public, and originally published in *The Saturday Evening Post* (Philadelphia), a weekly paper with the largest circulation in the world - over two million copies'.

During the process of its growth from a modest country house to its present proportions, Comarques has gained the reputation of having had more money spent on it during the last thirty years than any other house in the district.

By the kind permission of the present owners, Mrs. Bennett has had a tablet fixed on the brick wall immediately over the front entrance, bearing the inscription, 'Enoch Arnold Bennett, Author, lived here, 1913-1921'.

It was unveiled on the 5th of July, 1931, by Mr. Hugh Walpole, who in the course of his address expressed the opinion that Arnold Bennett spent the most tranquil years of his life at Comarques, adding that the memorial was a manifestation of personal feelings from Mrs. Arnold Bennett.

46. WAR ON TWO FRONTS

When Bennett and Marguerite moved into Comarques in April 1913 he was at the height of his fame and fortune, and understandably optimistic about the future. Writing to Mrs. Elsie Herzog in December 1912 he wrote that 'We now possess an early Queen Ann house near the Essex coast, and in February we are going to install ourselves there definitely for everlasting'. Not quite. Reading his *Journals* it is clear that the locality had its attractions, not least the coastline and the opportunities afforded to sail his boat *The Velsa,* bringing a sort of resigned acceptance of his new life:

> Walking last night for exercise along the Station road (6.30 p.m.) I saw the light of Clacton (not the lights - the light) and of Frinton, over the brows; a reflection in the sky ... Idea of a desolate coast (relatively) with the human settlements rather precariously here and there upon it. Darkness everywhere and just those lights on the clouds from below. Sense of the adventure of living on the earth at all; and of the essential similarity of all human existence. Idiocy of loathing or scorning a different kind of existence from your own; e.g. my attitude towards the primness of Frinton and its golf-club.[162]

And yet. An entry a mere week later suggests there is cause to doubt the truth of Bennett's sanguine attitude: 'Deranged slightly all week with a chill on the colon'.

Marriott's sun-dappled description of time spent at Comarques, together with Hugh Walpole's opinion that 'Bennett spent the most tranquil years of his life at Comarques', is at odds with the known facts. In large part the shadow that fell across Comarques was due to the outbreak of war and the unforeseen strain this put upon Bennett's finances. His friend and protégé, the young South African writer Pauline Smith, was a frequent visitor who witnessed at first hand the changing atmosphere:

> Into none of my later memories of Comarques does there come again the tranquillity and charm of those lovely summer days, or the sense of ease in friendship that was born of them. When next I went down to stay there, after my return from Africa, all was changed, and the peace of the old Georgian house and its garden, and of the little village beyond its gates, had fled with the peace of the world. Everywhere about and upon us now was the stir and strain, the upheaval and confusion of the business of war - the training-camps surrounded us, troops were quartered in the village, officers were billeted in the house, horses filled the stables.[163]

But far more disruptive, and ultimately destructive, than the war with Germany was the near remorseless domestic war fought out between an overworked and increasingly unreasonably irritable husband and a lonely and emotionally neglected wife. There may have been a facade of marital well-being maintained for friends and visitors but behind the scenes all was far from harmonious, with Bennett resorting to passing Marguerite a series of hand-written notes to express his dissatisfaction with household management:

> Quarrels between you and me will never happen if I am left at peace in my sleep, my work, and the organisation of the garden, which I direct. Your misfortune and mine is that with the best of intentions you forget. A quarrel has already developed about the maids, whom you have instructed to get up at 5.30, I complained; I explained to you at length that I couldn't do with it, and you changed it at once. But it appears to have started again. I again complained, but this time you were more obdurate. You told me that if I could neither sleep nor work, so much the worse - that it was absolutely necessary for the maids to get up at 5.30. So that the maids shan't be inconvenienced and the house managed according to programme, you have even suggested that I leave this house which exits

exclusively for me! Naturally in the end your commonsense prevailed ... It's absurd. It's absolutely as though my peace of mind, my work, my sleep, counted for nothing ...I give definite instructions. Immediately, without anyone having told me what's going on, my instructions are countermanded ... It cannot continue.[164]

After her visit, Mrs. Belloc-Lowndes wrote that Bennett had 'no knowledge of how an English country house ought to be run, and he compelled his wife to manage Comarques exactly as his mother had managed her small house in the Five Towns'.[165] The rift between husband and wife only continued to widen, with petty disputes about the arranging of furniture, to fierce arguments about the role of their gardener Lockyer, hated by Marguerite but valued by Bennett for his continued presence at a time of conscription; the full exchange of correspondence reads like a domestic drama by August Strindberg.

Arguably, the one positive legacy of this period is the lasting fictional record of key moments as seen through Bennett's eyes. For example, 'The Muscovy Ducks',[166] published in July 1915, casts Bennett as the peace-maker between Marguerite and Lockyer when the head-gardener kills one of a pair of her pet Muscovy ducks. Feeling increasingly isolated, Marguerite had acquired a number of pet animals, including two dogs, rabbits, cats, and a flock of ducks to assuage her loneliness. The ducks in particular caused Bennett constant irritation: 'I had already had them taken away from the lake because they kept me awake ... But we had to go through it all over again. One duck, then two, then several. And again I can't sleep because of them.... I give definite orders. Straight away, without anyone saying a word to me, my orders are cancelled'.[167] Clearly murder was on his mind, if only to be realised in the form of fictional displacement.

If Marriott is to believed, this domestic disharmony went undetected by his adopted daughter, Menetta, who shared only her father's enjoyment of 'delightful times' at Comarques. Born in 1908, Menetta would have been a young child when she visited Comarques, and given her father's cheerful nature, shielded from any adult disharmony. There is, though, an uncanny similarity between Bennett's unofficial adoption of his brother's son Richard, and Marriott's adoption of his sister Lucy's child. Several members of Marriott's family emigrated to Australia, and Lucy married into the Taylor family, giving birth to two other children apart from

Menetta. Menetta went on to marry Stanley Wainwright Morgan (1912-2002) in London, with whom she appeared on stage as a soprano, having been trained by Melba, accompanied on piano by her husband. Menetta's later professional success could not have been foreseen by Bennett, who, in a letter of 1929 written to his nephew Richard was less than complementary about her talent:

> However, I must tell you that Menetta Marriott is giving 'an hour of song' at FM's studio soon, & I much fear that I shall have to go there. She has absolutely no artistic feeling, & her performances are appalling. The power of suburbanism. But the Marriotts are terribly proud of her. It will be an infliction of a powerful intensity. I shall be ill if I can.[168]

Had news of Bennett's opinion reached Menetta's ears she may have taken some comfort in knowing that he had been even more damningly critical of Marguerite's ambition to recite poetry to the troops billeted in Thorpe-le- Soken during World War 1. It is, of course, thanks to Menetta, who died age 93 in 2002, that we have access to her father's memoir housed at Keele University.

Steps to Lake, Comarques. Watercolour on paper.

47. ROME

With the approach of Easter in 1912, my wife and I had decided to go to Rome for our holiday, partly because our friend Gilbert Ledward the sculptor was studying there. He had gained the valuable scholarship for sculpture awarded by the British School, which provided an ample maintenance allowance and a free studio.

Arnold Bennett was at that time cruising on his yacht in the Gulf of Genoa, and was at the various ports along the Italian coast. We had received several characteristic post cards from him, one of which was from Genoa.

I addressed a letter to reach him there, telling him of our holiday plans, and he wrote asking me to send him the name of the hotel we should be staying at in Rome, and said he would meet us there. His wife, who didn't so much enjoy yachting, with the attendant distressing effects of rough weather, was making the journey over-land in her car.

A holiday in Rome at any time is desirable, but in such congenial company, and sharing the combined luxuries of a yacht and a motor car made it doubly enjoyable. They had already reached Rome by the time we got there, and we found a letter waiting at our hotel asking us to notify them as soon as we arrived; which we did immediately.

Next morning we called on Gilbert Ledward and arranged a time for all of us to visit his studio and view the work he was engaged upon. Shortly afterwards Mrs. Bennett came with the car and conducted us to the yacht, and we found Bennett on board clothed in the approved manner of an owner yachtsman.

While we were being shown over the yacht, I was astonished at the amount of accommodation it provided in a comparatively small space, and the ingenuity displayed in the design of the furniture and fitments caused me to wonder why similar space-saving devices weren't used in dwellings, and I secretly resolved to adopt some of them on my return. (I did in fact go to several London firms which specialised in ships furniture when I got back, but I found their wares were beyond my means.) The yacht was anchored in a bend of the Tiber, and paintable subjects could be seen from the deck on all sides, so Bennett and I spent several mornings sketching where we could be free from the irritating attentions of street urchins and loafers. We lunched on board, and afterwards we all drove in the car to places of interest in the city and suburbs.

It was a notable experience to traverse in a modern motor-car the ancient Appian Way to the catacombs, the subterranean burial places of the first Roman Christians, and the burial place of St. Cecilia. All very impressive.

Other excursions by car included Tivoli, where stands the Villa d'Este and the ruins of Hadrian's Villa near at hand. We also went to one of the most picturesque of hill towns; St. Benedict's town Subiaco, where the first Italian printing press was established. Bennett and I promised ourselves we would visit it again for the purpose of sketching but unfortunately the promise was never fulfilled on his part, though I have since done work there.

One night Bennett booked a box at the Opera House for a gala performance of Rossini's opera *The Barber of Seville,* which was attended by the king of Italy. Shortly before the opera commenced we were startled by an outburst of hissing and other demonstrations of displeasure in various parts of the house, but chiefly from the gallery, and we discovered that the cause was the arrival in one of the boxes of a number of ladies wearing violent wigs of brilliant colour; emerald green, vermilion, violet and orange. The hostile demonstrations were so persistent, that the ladies were ultimately compelled to retire from the scene.

To my mind, the performance of the opera was superb, and I was unable to agree with Bennett's patriotic view that it had been better done at Covent Garden; but his judgment was probably correct.

The time at our disposal was too short to allow of much being devoted to churches. Indeed Rome has so many churches that to have given them adequate attention would have absorbed all our time, so we had to be content with a not very thorough examination of St. Peter's.

After leaving St. Peter's we entered the Vatican where the work of Michelangelo in the Sistine Chapel claimed most of our attention. I had to confess to a feeling of disappointment on entering this private chapel of the Popes. It was so much smaller than I had imagined it to be. The prodigious personality of Michelangelo overwhelmed and dwarfed it. The immense crowd of insistent passionate figures covering the walls seemed to reflect his annoyance at being forced to forsake for so long a time his true vocation, sculpture.

These 16th century decorations failed to convey the spiritual significance which the church decorations by the 14th century painters succeeded in imparting, and it was to me both spiritual and physical torture to look intently up to the painted ceiling of the chapel, where the finely designed sculpturesque figures of the prophets, sibyls, and slaves are placed in sham architectural settings, all achieved in paint. My criticisms evoked no echo of agreement from Bennett who was profoundly impressed by the nobility and grandeur of the compositions; so Michelangelo's great reputation remained resplendent.

Other places of interest we visited in the city included the Forum, the Capitoline Museum and Picture Gallery, the Borghesi Palace, Museum and Gardens, and the Coliseum; the latter by moonlight, which made it the more romantic under the effect of subdued lights and rich sombre shadows.

We visited Gilbert Ledward's studio, and Bennett took such a keen interest in the work he saw in progress, that I quite expected he would be adding modelling to his other artistic hobbies, but I never heard of his doing so.

If our engagements in London had permitted of an extension of the holiday, we should have accepted Bennett's tempting invitation for my wife and I to divide, she to make the return journey with Mrs. Bennett by car, while I shared the amenities of the yacht. But unfortunately this could not be done.

47. WHEN IN ROME

Marriott's reference to visiting the studio of Gilbert Ledward (1888-1960) passes over his and Bennett's close personal connections with the family of a sculptor of some renown. Gilbert's mother, Mary Jane Wood, was a descendant of the famous Burslem Wood family of potters. Her eldest child, Anne, married William Kennerley, and their son, William Wood Kennerley (born in 1870) became Bennett's brother-in-law in 1903 when he married his favourite sister, Tertia Bennett. Beyond those basic facts, navigating the maze of Bennett-Kennerley-Wood interpersonal relations is probably best left to someone with more genealogical knowledge that I possess! Catherine Goodwin's wide-ranging essay on 'Arnold Bennett, Sculpture and Sculptors' emphasises the important role played by Marriott in shaping Ledward's early career: 'At the age of seven, around 1895, he had his portrait painted by Frederick Marriott. Educated at St.Marks College, Chelsea, Gilbert moved to Germany with his family in 1901. By 1902, Gilbert had returned and under the guidance of Frederick Marriott, continued his art education, winning a scholarship to Chelsea Polytechnic'.[169]

In August 1912 Bennett invited Ledward to join his party on his private yacht, *Velsa*, exploring the canals and estuaries of Belgium and Holland. Writing home to Marguerite, Bennett shows little sympathy for a novice sailor who encounters rain in buckets, high winds and storms, and needs sea-sickness medicine:

> Gilbert is amazed by the trip. I can tell you that he is a charming boy but fairly worthless. He knows nothing, even artistically. He has backward ideas, and never has the faintest spark of originality. He is a perfect travelling companion. But I am disappointed in him. I thought him better. If he really is, or will be, he is either hiding it out of shyness, or else he is decidedly nor precocious. But I am sure he is not.[170]

Thirteen days later and little has changed despite Bennett claiming to have 'taught him a great deal'. What is surprising, given our knowledge of Ledward's future achievements, is Bennett's report of his claiming that 'I only began to take an interest in art last year' and 'had not considered sculpture as an emotional art'.[171] It is tempting to read Ledward's responses as a deprecatory self-effacing defence mechanism faced with the over-whelming confidence and personality of the older man on whose largesse he was temporally dependent.

And then something must have changed, for Ledward went on to produce several sculptures of Marguerite, and more significantly, was commissioned by the Ministry of Information, where Bennett had some influence, to design a relief depicting the British army at the Battle of the Marne. Indeed, Ledward was in great demand as a respected and influential sculptor of war memorials . By the end of his career, Ledward had totally demolished Bennett's over-hasty unsympathetic pen-portrait:

In later life, Ledward was Professor of Sculpture at the Royal College of Art (1927-1929) and in 1934 established his company Sculptured Memorials and Headstones, which promoted the better design of memorials in English churchyards. He was elected as a Royal Academician in 1937, was President of the Royal Society of British Sculptors from 1954-1956 and became a Trustee of the Royal Academy in 1956. The Potteries Museum & Art Gallery has an archive of material relating to Gilbert Ledward, consisting of original sketches, plans and notebooks.[172]

A thread which neatly leads us back to The Potteries and the Museum, which holds an important Bennett archive, as well as maintaining a permanent Bennett display, and which in 2019 mounted an exhibition of his young friend's work, *Visions in Stone: Gilbert Ledward RA - sculpture and drawings* . This display of Ledward's sculptures in stone and bronze, as well as his drawings and design portfolios, was part of the 250th anniversary celebrations of the Royal Academy. There is also a postcard in Keele University's Bennett archive which creates a thread linking Bennett, Marriott, Ledward, and Rome. On 12 April 1914 Bennett sent a postcard - 'We have been weather-bound at Elba for 3 days' -- to Marriott, care of Gilbert Ledward at the British School in Rome.

Bennett's later letters and journals are replete with references to Rome and the Mediterranean. His 1928 limited edition travel volume *Mediterranean Scenes: Rome, Greece, Constantinople* has a chapter on 'Easter Day in Rome' in which people watching takes precedence over cultural sites/sights. Visiting the church at Santa Maria Maggiore it 'was the demeanour of people in churches on this day that I wanted to see'.[173] And their demeanour is clinically exposed as one of 'vacant curiosity' not helped by 'mediocre organ-playing and very bad, perfunctory singing'. Bennett, the almost obsessive recorder of the cruel passage from youth to old age, finds himself arrested by an eschatological example of their failure to connect:

> On either side of a closed confessional-box two girls were waiting for a priest. They were nicely dressed, with some style, and had a contrite and perturbed air. At another confessional-box were another couple of similar girls, kneeling close to the woodwork and hiding their faces in their hands. And as I passed by I had a glimpse inside the box an aged, harsh, austere priest, embittered by life, and, I should say, suffering from tedium. He was attending to neither of his penitents. He was looking about; he looked at me. [174]

But once on the road Bennett usually finds reason to take pleasure in his surroundings, and Rome is no exception:

> I take a Victoria (iron tyres), and clatter round behind something on four hoofs, and am continually noticing beauties and interests that I have never noticed before, though I have seen sights in Rome for months together. Rome is endless; it has more attractions than any other city to anybody with a feeling for either art or history or religion.[175]

Perhaps the best and most colourful fictional portrait of Rome painted by Bennett occurs in his 1927 novel *The Vanguard*. Its manifold attractions are made abundantly clear: '"Anything to do in Rome this evening?'" Lord Furber demanded. The head waiter bristled at a question so nearly bordering on an insult to Rome, his Rome. He catalogued the opera, eight other theatres, and some sixteen cinemas, besides a music-hall, and a nocturnal ceremonial in one of the churches'.[176]   The novel itself is underrated, being taken at face-value as a fantasia or entertainment, when close reading reveals Bennett's insider's knowledgeable exposure of suspect financial and press manipulation, of modernity on the precipice of what will become the Great Depression. More significant from a literary perspective is my belief that this novel breaks new ground by making the growing popularity of home-movies among the upper-class at leisure an important part of the plot, whilst also signalling their insidious potential for fostering the sort of reputational damage now so prevalent on social media.

Subiaco at Night, colour etching, published 1 June 1919: 'We also went to one   of the most picturesque of hill towns.'

Marriott's St.Cecilia, 1903: '... to traverse in a motor-car the ancient Appian way to the catacombs ... and the burial place of St. Cecilia. All very impressive'.

49. BENNETT'S DEATH

And now alas, Arnold Bennett has passed from our midst, and a vital literary force has been prematurely removed in the zenith of his powers.

His untimely death on the twenty seventh of March, 1931, occurred after an illness of seven weeks duration. At first his illness gave no cause for anxiety, and there was every expectation that he would make a rapid recovery, but as the weeks passed, and it became definitely known that he was suffering from typhoid fever, the extreme gravity of his condition was realised, and blood transfusions were resorted to in the hope of saving his life, but he gradually weakened, and after a period of unconsciousness, death intervened.

Seldom has the nation been more deeply stirred than by the news of the illness and death of this brilliant man. To his many friends the effect of the blow was terrific.

Articles acclaiming his genius and great achievements appeared in the columns of every important newspaper in the land, and in some of them it was suggested that he should be given the supreme honour of burial in Westminster Abbey. It is universally taught that there is no one who cannot be replaced, yet it will be difficult indeed to fill Arnold Bennett's place in the wide circle of his friends, or in the wider world of book-lovers outside. His death spread sadness throughout the artistic communities in which he had been such a prominent figure.

For the last twenty-five years of his life he was constantly in the full glare of the public eye, and his many interests and activities outside his own profession were well known.

Wherever anything of exceptional interest was going on he was always in attendance, and by the impelling force of his striking personality he was a centre of interest at concerts, operas, art exhibitions and the first nights of new plays.

He was one of the most consistently industrious writers of this generation, and was never deterred by the magnitude of any task he embarked upon, even though it came amidst a multitude of other avocations.

He recorded and interpreted the life of the Pottery towns of his native county with extraordinary lucidity, and as an analyst of the character of the people of that district he stands pre-eminent and unexcelled. Endowed with an impelling insatiable thirst for knowledge of every manifestation of life, he explored every avenue in pursuit of it, realising that it was the most important necessity of all who take up writing as a profession. He brought the inquisitive eye of a Pre-Raphaelite artist to bear on every complexity and phenomena the world around him presented, and he recorded the impressions he received in an exceptionally illuminating way.

His scrupulous attention to minute detail, as revealed in his books, has at times met with criticism, yet the detail was always relevant and handled in a masterly manner.

He had a deeply rooted objection to shams of all kinds, and was a stickler for truth and insisted on getting it.

It is generally conceded that Arnold Bennett was a great writer, a great artist, a great character, and a great man, and to those fortunate people who knew him intimately, he was an unfailingly generous and staunch friend.

50. LEAVE-TAKING

Marriott's final paragraph makes a fitting epitaph from a friend who knew him well. It is personal and heart-felt. And for those of us who never had the pleasure of his company there nevertheless remains the lasting legacy of his work in all its rich diversity to engage, challenge, delight and divert us. For, as the 8 April 1931 *Punch* valedictory[177] expressed it:

Here lies a man, from common clay descended,
Who took the common people of the clay
And from their lives of grime and greatness blended
Created Life that shall not pass away.

ACKNOWLEDGEMENTS

Through the good offices of George Beardmore, Arnold Bennett's nephew, Keele University Library acquired the unpublished manuscript of Frederick Marriott's memoir *My association with Arnold Bennett* from his daughter Menetta, Mrs Wainwright Morgan. It was first reproduced as a booklet in Bennett's centenary birth year of 1967, but with a number of passages omitted. These are now included in the present volume, and I gratefully acknowledge Keele University's permission to publish the full manuscript, together with some Marriott images held in the Bennett Collection. In particular I wish to thank Helen Burton, Special Collection and Archives Administrator, who has extended every courtesy throughout my visits and been unfailingly helpful in locating documents and providing a hospitable space in which to study them.

The original holograph of *The Crime* is held in the Arnold Bennett Archive at the Potteries Museum & Art Gallery, Stoke-on-Trent, and I must thank Joseph Perry for giving permission to publish my transcription of it in this book. The Museum also holds the most extensive collection of Arnold Bennett watercolours, two of which are included in this study.

Nicholas Redman has once again been unfailingly generous and helpful in both providing important documentary evidence and in correcting those careless errors in my manuscript that less experienced eyes might have missed. It is, for example, thanks to Nicholas's personal Bennett archive that I have been able to include Bennett's Mrs. Roy Devereux's book review and reproduce his cover painting for *Carlotta*.

Amanda Bromley, the owner of Barewall Gallery in Burslem, Stoke-on-Trent, is to be unhesitatingly congratulated for mounting the retrospective exhibition of Frederick Marriott's etchings which initially inspired my research. Carole Williams first directed me to on-line ancestry sites. Jenny Graveson has performed invaluable service and advice in tracking down details of Bennett and Marriott family histories. At one point she even telephoned me whilst on location outside the Fowl House, before sending me the rarely seen photograph of Bennett at the Fowl House reproduced in this volume. Alan Pedley kindly sent me the 1981 sale details for Marriott's Chelsea home.

Tim Crook, at Goldsmiths, University of London, helpfully drew my attention to his invaluable on-line *Goldsmiths History Project* which contains a wealth of information on Marriott's long-term connection with the

College. Etchings and paintings by Marriott, together with his official College portrait, are to be found there. Christopher Morton has kept up a helpful exchange of emails with me over some twelve months. Alan Grobler was very helpful in sending me his article on Frank Pickford Marriott, included in *Looking Back*, the journal of the Historical Society of Port Elizabeth, South Africa. Mary Beardmore gave me information on Trinity Hall. Christine Till has been unfailingly supportive and encouraging throughout the time I have been engrossed in writing this book.

Finally, I owe an enormous debt of gratitude to Bruce Richardson and Churnet Valley Books. I have worked with Bruce for the past 15 years, in which time we have published no less than 19 books together, including newly discovered Arnold Bennett novels and stories, and a major study of Melvyn Bragg's Cumbrian novels. In his quietly unassuming way, Bruce's publishing company has significantly added to our knowledge of Bennett's importance as a towering figure of English literature.

I have endeavoured to acknowledge the source of the many contributions in either the main body of the text or in the Notes, and apologise if anyone has slipped through the net. Whilst every effort has been made to trace and contact the holders of copyright material the publisher would be grateful to know of any omissions.

NOTES

1 George Eliot. *Middlemarch*. Harmondsworth, Middlesex: Penguin Books,1965]1871], p.896.

2 References kindly emailed by Nicholas Redman

3 Kate Mosse. *The Burning Chambers*. London: Pan Macmillan, 2018

4 Kate Mosse. *Labyrinth*, London: Orion, 2005.

5 Holderness, Graham, quoted in Jane McVeigh, *In Collaboration with British Literary Biography: Haunting Conversations*. Cham, Switzerland: Palgrave MacMillan,2018, p.10.

6 Alan Grobler. 'Frank Pickford Marriott, A.R.C.A. A Post Pre-Raphaelite' in *Kykies In Die Verlede*. Port Elizabeth: Historical Society of Port Elizabeth, 2008.

7 Ibid., p.24.

8 Bennett renamed the five towns of Tunstall, Burslem, Hanley, Stoke, and Longton as Turnhill, Bursley, Hanbridge, Knype and Longshaw respectively.

9 Charlotte Higgins. *Red Thread: On Mazes & Labyrinths*. London: Jonathan Cape,2018, p.144.

10 Alice Clapp-Itnyre. *British Hymn Books for Children: 1800-1900*. London: Aldgate, 2016.

11 I am indebted to Chris Morton for bringing this article to my attention.

12 Frank Swinnerton. *Arnold Bennett: A Last Word*, London: Hamish Hamilton), 1978.

13 Ibid., p.35.

14 Ibid., p.36.

15 Philippe Garner. 'Unpublished Notes on Gesso by Frederick Marriott' in *The Bulletin of the Decorative Arts Society 1890-1940'*, Number 1, 1977, pp.28-35.

16 Ibid., p.28.

17 Ibid., p.30.

18 Ibid., p.35.

19 Ibid., p.33.

20 For full details see James Hepburn, edited, *Letters of Arnold Bennett, Volume 1, Letters to J. B. Pinker*. London: Oxford University Press, 1966, pp.405-6.

21 Estate agent Marks's property particulars were kindly sent me by Alan Pedley.

22 Margaret Drabble. *Arnold Bennett: a biography*. London: Weidenfeld & Nicolson,1974, p.56.

23 Arnold Bennett. *The Truth about an Author*. London: Archibald Constable, 1903, pp.54-5.

24 Arnold Bennett. *The Journals of Arnold Bennett, Volume 1, 1896-1910*. Edited Newman Flower. London: Cassell & Company, 1932, p.84.

25 Ibid., p.63.

26 Arnold Bennett. *The Grim Smile of the Five Towns*. London: Chapman and Hall, 1907, p.216.

27 Harris Wilson, edited, *Arnold Bennett & H.G.Wells: A Record of a Personal and a Literary Friendship*. Urbana, U.S.A: University of Illinois Press,1960, pp.36-7.

28 *Arnold Bennett. Sketches for Autobiography,* edited by James Hepburn. London: George Allen & Unwin,1979,p.38.

29 *The Truth about an Author*, p.58

30 Arnold Bennett. *Lord Dover & Other Lost Stories,* edited by John Shapcott. Leek: Churnet Valley Books, 2011, p.7.

31 Ibid.,p.8.

32 J.Madison Davis, edited, *Conversations with Robertson Davies*. London: University Press of Mississippi, 1989, pp.253-4.

33 Martin Laux. 'The Relationship between Arnold Bennett and Pauline Smith' in The Thirteenth Annual Arnold Bennett Conference: *Arnold Bennett: Friends and Acquaintances,* 2017, edited by Chitose Ikawa and Randi Saloman, Stoke-on-Trent: Arnold Bennett Society, p.24.

34 Pauline Smith. *A.B. .... a minor marginal note.* London: Jonathan Cape, 1933, pp.1-14

35 Ibid, pp.14-15

36 Claire Buck, edited, *Women's Literature A-Z*. London: Bloomsbury, 1994.

37 Quoted in Andrew Harrison. *The Life of D.H. Lawrence*. Chichester: Wiley Blackwell, 2016, p.170.

38 *Letters of Arnold Bennett, Volume 1: Letters to J.B. Pinker*, edited by James Hepburn.London:Oxford University Press, 1966, p.259.

39 Ibid., p.260.

40 Quoted in John Shapcott, 'Aesthetics for Everyman: Arnold Bennett's Evening Standard Columns', in *Middlebrow literary Cultures*, edited by Erica Brown and Mary Grover, New York: Palgrave Macmillan, 2012,p.93.

41 Quoted in Michael Foot, *The History of Mr. Wells*. Washington,D.C.,U.S.A.: Counterpoint,1995, p.33.

42 *The Journals of Arnold Bennett, Volume 1*, pp39-40.

43 Ibid., pp.38-9.

44 Ibid., p.36.

45 Ibid., p.80.

46 Ibid.

47 Ibid.

48 Arnold Bennett. *Arnold Bennett's Uncollected Short Stories, 1892-1932,* edited by John Shapcott. Leek: Churnet Valley Books, 2010.

49 Arnold Bennett. *Fame and Fiction*. London: Grant Richards, 1901,p.73.

50 Ibid., p.75.

51 Ann Heilmann. *New Woman Strategies: Sarah Grand, Olive Schriener, Mona Caird*. Manchester: Manchester University Press, 2004, p.22. As well as including the pictures of Grand's home, Heilmann's book offers an in-depth analysis of Grand's presentation of self in interviews.

52 Reginald Pound. The *Strand magazine: 1891-1950*. London: William Heinemann, 1966, p.105.

53 Arnold Bennett. *The Woman Who Stole Everything and other stories*. London: Cassell and Company,1927, p.46.

54 *The Truth about an Author*, p.21.

55 Ibid., pp.23-5.

56 *The Journals of Arnold Bennett*. New York: The Literary Guild, 1933, p.484.

57 Cyril Ionides and J.B.Atkins. *A Floating Home*. London: Chatto & Windus, 1918, p.150.

58 There are two excellent studies of Bennett as artist: Nicholas Redman, 'Arnold Bennett, watercolourist, etcher & sketcher' in, edited by Alan Pedley, *The Arnold Bennett Society Newsletter, Volume 5, No.6*, Stoke-on-Trent: Arnold Bennett Society, 2014, pp.29-39; Catherine Goodwin, 'Bennett and Art, in, edited by John Shapcott, *An Arnold Bennett Companion*, Leek: Churnet Valley Books, 2015, pp.79-105.

59 John Shapcott, edited, *Arnold Bennett Companion Volume 11*. Leek: Churnet Valley Books, 2017, p.25. See also Randi Saloman's essay, '"But luck was in everything": The Architecture of Arnold Bennett's *Clayhanger* novels', pp.188-208.

60 *Letters of Arnold Bennett, Volume 1*, p.271.

61 Arnold Bennett. *The Roll-Call*. London: Hutchinson & Co., 1918, p.1.

62 *The Art of E.A.Rickards*, London: Technical Journals Ltd., p.5.

63 Ibid.

64 *The Journals of Arnold Bennett, Volume 1*, pp.111-12.

65 *The Roll-Call*, pp.25-6.

66 Ibid., p.27.

67 Arnold Bennett. *Your United States*. New York: Harper & Brothers, 1912, p.50.

68 Arnold Bennett. *Over There: War Scenes on the Western Front*. New York: A.L.Burt Company, 1915, p.85.

69 *The Potteries Museum & Art Gallery, Local History Collection*, STKMG: 1953.SH.65(j). Collection,

70 Reginald Pound. *Arnold Bennett*. London: Heinemann, 1952, p.81.

71 Ibid., pp.82-3.

72 For a comprehensive study of Bennett's musical heritage, see R.Nettle, *Music in the Five Towns: 1840-1914*, London: Oxford University Press, 1944.

73 *Letters of Arnold Bennett, Volume 11*, p.100 (Note 61).

74 *The Journals of Arnold Bennett, Volume 1*, p.32.

75 Ibid.

76 Ibid., p.87.

77 Arnold Bennett. *The Ghost*. London: Chatto & Windus, 1907, pp.16-7.

78 Arnold Bennett. *The Grim Smile of the Five Towns*. London: Chapman & Hall, 1907, p.145.

79 Ibid., p.159.

80 Arnold Bennett. *Punch and Judy,* edited by John Shapcott, Leek: Churnet Valley Books, 2012, p.88.

81 For a detailed description of the circumstances surrounding Bennett's film scenario see my 'Introduction' to Arnold Bennett's *The Wedding Dress*. Leek: Churnet Valley Books, 2013.

82 Arnold Bennett. *Piccadilly,* edited by John Shapcott. Leek: Churnet Valley Books, 2017, p.15.

83 Arnold Bennett. *Punch and Judy*, p.5.

84 Reprinted in Arnold Bennett, *The Savour of Life*. London: Cassell and Company, 1928, p.146.

85 Marguerite Bennett (Mrs. Arnold Bennett). *Arnold Bennett*. New York: Adelphi Company, 1925, p.14.

86 Georges Lafourcade. *Arnold Bennett: A Study*. London: Frederick Muller, 1939, p.16.

87 Arnold Bennett. *The Truth about an Author*, pp.80-1.

88 *The Journals of Arnold Bennett, Volume 1, p.43.*

89 Ibid.

90 Arnold Bennett. *The Strange Vanguard*. London: Cassell, 1928, p.63.

91 Arnold Bennett. *The Loot of Cities*. London: Alston Rivers, 1905, p.92.

92 Ibid.

93 Ibid., p.93.

94 Nicholas Redman. 'Bennett in Algeria', in *The Arnold Bennett Society Newsletter, Volume 4, No. 18*, edited by Alan Pedley, Stoke: Arnold Bennett Society, 2012, pp.11-24.

95 *Letters of Arnold Bennett, Volume 1*, p.48.

96 Walter Benjamin. *The Arcades Project*. Massachusetts, U.S.A.: Belknap Press of Harvard University Press, 1999, p.3.

97 Arnold Bennett. *Hugo: A Fantasia on Modern Themes*. New York: F. M. Buckles and Company, 1906, p.121.

98 Ibid., p.165.

99 Ibid., p.236.

100 *Letters of Arnold Bennett, Volume 11*, p.138.

101 Ibid., p.139.

102 Ibid., p.164.

103 *Letters of Arnold Bennett, Volume 111,1916-1931*, edited by James Hepburn. London: Oxford University Press, 1970, p.228.

104 Arnold Bennett. *Teresa of Watling Street*. London: Chatto & Windus, 1904, p. 100.

105 Harris Wilson, edited, *Arnold Bennett and H.G.Wells: A Record of a Personal and a Literary Friendship*. Urbana, USA: University of Illonois Press, 1960, p.77.

106 Ibid., p.78.

107 Ibid., p.90.

108 *The Journals of Arnold Bennett, Volume 1*, p.54.

109 Ibid.

110 Ibid.

111 Ibid., p.56.

112 Ibid.

113 *The Journals of Arnold Bennett, Volume 1*, p.235.

114 *Letters of Arnold Bennett, Volume 11*, p.208.

115 Ibid.

116 *Letters of Arnold Bennett, Volume 11*, Note, p.210

117 Ibid. , p.211.

118 Ibid., p.215.

119 Ibid.

120 Georges Lafourcade. *Arnold Bennett: A Study*. London: Frederick Muller Ltd, 1939, p.41-2.

121 *Letters of Arnold Bennett, Volume 11*, p.216.

122 *Letters of Arnold Bennett, Volume 1V*, Family letters, edited by James Hepburn. London: Oxford University Press, 1986, p.31.

123 Ibid., pp.32-3.

124 Dudley Barker. *Writer by Trade: A view of Arnold Bennett*. London: Geo. Allen & Unwin, 1966, pp.194-201.

125 *Letters of Arnold Bennett, Volume 1V*, p.33.

126 *The Journals of Arnold Bennett, Volume 1*, p.261.

127 Ibid.

128 Ibid.

129 Letter quoted in *Reginald Pound, Arnold Bennett*, p.187.

130 *The Journals of Arnold Bennett, Volume 1*, p.272.

131 Derek Hyde. *New-found Voices: Women in Nineteenth-Century English Music*. London: Routledge, 2018.

132 A recording of 'The Devout Lover' can be downloaded from Hyperion's *In Praise of Women 1993* album at www.hyperion-records.co.uk.

133 *Letters of Arnold Bennett, Volume 1V*, p.23.

134 *The Journals of Arnold Bennett, Volume 1*, p.244.

135 There is no extended critical examination of Bennett's sparse poetic output. The only document of which I am aware is Paul Plant's self published monograph, *Arnold Bennett: A Poet of the Ordinary, March 2000*.

136 Kurt Koenigsberger. 'Bennett's Books and Manuscripts: The Aesthetics of Objects', in *An Arnold Bennett Companion*, edited by John Shapcott, Leek: Churnet Valley Books, 2015, p.56.

137 *Letters of Arnold Bennett, Volume 1V*, p.35.

138 Ibid., p.32.

139 *The Journals of Arnold Bennett, Volume 1*, pp.245-6.

140 *Letters of Arnold Bennett, Volume 1*, p.97.

141 Arnold Bennett. *The Old Wives' Tale*. London: Ernest Benn, 1927, pp.V-V1.

142 Arnold Bennett, 'From a French Journal', in *Life and Letters*, edited by Desmond MacCarthy, p.24.

143 Arnold Bennett. *The Glimpse*. London: Chapman & Hall, 1909. p.179.

144 *The Journals of Arnold Bennett, Volume 1*, pp.139-40.

NOTES

145 The complete list of dedications reads: *A Man from the North* - Sarah Bennett; *Anna of the Five Towns* - Herbert Sharpe; *A Great Man* - Frederick Marriott; *Tales of the Five Towns* - Marcel Schwob; *Sacred and Profane Love* - Eden Phillpotts; *Whom God Hath Joined* - Roy Devereux; *The Grim Smile of the Fie Towns* - Joseph Dawson; *Buried Alive* - John Frederick Farrer; *The Old Wives' Tale* - W.W.K; *Imperial Palace* - George Reeves-Smith.

146 Reginald Pound, p.49.

147 Barry Howarth. *The Craft of Arnold Bennett*. Unpublished PhD thesis, University of Liverpool, 2016, pp.148-9.

148 *Letters of Arnold Bennett, Volume 1V*, p.xx.

149 *The Journals of Arnold Bennett, Volume 1*, pp.104-5.

150 Ann Heilmann. *The late-Victorian Marriage Question: A Collection of Key Texts*. London: Routledge 2000 p.106

151 Talia Schaffer. *The Forgotten Female Aesthetes: Literary Culture in Late-Victorian England.* University of Virginia Press, p.111

152 My thanks to Nicholas Redman for sending me a copy of Bennett's review.

153 Catherine Goodwin. 'Bennett and Art', in *An Arnold Bennett Companion*, p.83.

154 *The Arnold Bennett Collection: Volume 2, documents and letters, plays, and manuscripts, books.* Stoke-on-Trent: The Potteries Museum & Art Gallery, 2008.

155 *The Letters of Arnold Bennett, Volume 11*, p.145

156 Ibid., p.130.

157 *Letters of Arnold Bennett, Volume 1V*, p.151, translation by James Hepburn.

158 Quoted in John Lucas, *Arnold Bennett: A Study of his Fiction*, London: Methuen,1974, p.91.

159 *The Journals of Arnold Bennett, Volume 1*, p.31

160 John Wain. *The Contenders.*, London: Macmillan & Co, 1958, pp.4-5.

161 *The Journals of Arnold Bennett, Volume 111*, p.239.

162 *The Journals of Arnold Bennett, Volume 11*, pp.73-4.

163 Pauline Smith. *A.B.: '.... a minor marginal note'*. London: Jonathan Cape, 1933, p.41.

164 Quoted in *Arnold Bennett in Love: Arnold Bennett and his wife Marguerite Soulié, a correspondence,* edited & translated by George & Jean Beardmore. London: David Bruce & Watson, 1972, p.72.

165 Ibid., p.73.

166 Arnold Bennett. 'The Muscovy Ducks', reprinted in *Arnold Bennett's Uncollected Short stories, 1892-1932*, edited by John Shapcott, Leek: Churnet Valley Books, 2010.

167 *Letters of Arnold Bennett, Volume 1V*, p.129.

168 Ibid., p.575.

169 Catherine Goodwin. 'Arnold Bennett, Sculpture and Sculptors', in *Arnold Bennett Companion, Volume 11,* edited by John Shapcott. Leek: Churnet Valley Books, 2017, p.177.

170 *Letters of Arnold Bennett, Volume 1V*, p.101.

171 Ibid., p.102.

172 Catherine Goodwin, *Arnold Bennett Companion, Volume 11*, p.180.

173 Arnold Bennett. *Mediterranean Scenes: Rome, Greece, Constantinople*. London: Cassell & Co 1928, p.17.

174 Ibid., p.16.

175 Ibid., p.23.

176 Arnold Bennett. *The Strange Vanguard*, New York: The literary Guild of America, 1927, p.115.

177 For the full text of the valedictory, see Pound, *Arnold Bennett*, p.368.